Kaplan Publishing are constantly finding nev
looking for exam success and our online res
extra dimension to your studies.

CW01011386

This book comes with free MyKaplan online
study anytime, anywhere. **This free online resource is not sold
separately and is included in the price of the book.**

Having purchased this book, you have access to the following online study materials:

CONTENT	AAT	
	Text	Kit
Electronic version of the book	✓	✓
Knowledge Check tests with instant answers	✓	
Mock assessments online	✓	✓
Material updates	✓	✓

How to access your online resources

Received this book as part of your Kaplan course?

If you have a MyKaplan account, your full online resources will be added automatically, in line with the
information in your course confirmation email. If you've not used MyKaplan before, you'll be sent an activation
email once your resources are ready.

Bought your book from Kaplan?

We'll automatically add your online resources to your MyKaplan account. If you've not used MyKaplan before,
you'll be sent an activation email.

Bought your book from elsewhere?

Go to **www.mykaplan.co.uk/add-online-resources**
Enter the ISBN number found on the title page and back cover of this book.
Add the unique pass key number contained in the scratch panel below.
You may be required to enter additional information during this process to set up or confirm your account
details.

This code can only be used once for the registration of this book online. This registration and your online
content will expire when the examinations covered by this book have taken place. Please allow one hour from
the time you submit your book details for us to process your request.

Please scratch the film to access your unique code.

Please be aware that this code is case-sensitive and you will need
to include the dashes within the passcode, but not when entering
the ISBN.

PUBLISHING

AAT

PROFESSIONAL DIPLOMA IN ACCOUNTING

PDSY

FAMILIARISATION AND PRACTICE KIT
Argent Electric Motors Ltd (AEM Ltd)

This Exam Kit supports study for the following AAT qualifications:
AAT Level 4 Diploma in Professional Accounting
AAT Diploma in Professional Accounting at SCQF Level 8

British Library Cataloguing-in-Publication Data

A catalogue record for this book is available from the British Library.

Published by:

Kaplan Publishing UK

Unit 2 The Business Centre

Molly Millar's Lane

Wokingham

Berkshire

RG41 2QZ

ISBN: 978-1-83996-098-7

© Kaplan Financial Limited, 2022

Printed and bound in Great Britain.

CONTENTS

Live assessment pre-release material

This practice kit is based on the live assessment pre-release information for **Argent Electric Motors Ltd (AEM Ltd).** This is relevant for live assessments from **30 January 2023**.

Make sure you download and print a copy from the AAT website to use in conjunction with this kit.

Studying this material will encourage you to think about the assessment topics in an integrated way, which is necessary for performing well in the synoptic assessment.

Note: Kaplan authors have invented scenarios and additional details when writing questions based on the case. When sitting the live assessment, make sure you don't confuse what content is in the pre-release information and what additional details are in this practice kit.

You will find a wealth of other resources to help you with your studies on the AAT website:

www.aat.org.uk/

Quality and accuracy are of the utmost importance to us so if you spot an error in any of our products, please send an email to mykaplanreporting@kaplan.com with full details, or follow the link to the feedback form in MyKaplan.

Our Quality Co-ordinator will work with our technical team to verify the error and take action to ensure it is corrected in future editions.

SYNOPTIC ASSESSMENT

AAT AQ16 introduced a Synoptic Assessment, which students must complete if they are to achieve the appropriate qualification upon completion of a qualification. In the case of the Advanced Diploma in Accounting, students must pass all of the mandatory assessments and the Synoptic Assessment to achieve the qualification.

As a Synoptic Assessment is attempted following completion of individual units, it draws upon knowledge and understanding from those units. It may be appropriate for students to retain their study materials for individual units until they have successfully completed the Synoptic Assessment for that qualification.

Four units within the Professional Diploma in Accounting are mandatory. Of these, three are assessed individually in end of unit assessments, but this qualification also includes a synoptic assessment, sat towards the end of the qualification, which draws on and assesses knowledge and understanding from all four mandatory units:

- Financial statements of Limited Companies – end of unit assessment

- Management Accounting: Budgeting – end of unit assessment

- Management Accounting: Decision and Control – end of unit assessment

- Accounting Systems and Controls – assessed within the synoptic assessment only

Summary of learning outcomes from underlying units which are assessed in the synoptic assessment

Underlying unit	Learning outcomes required
Accounting Systems and Controls	LO1, LO2, LO3, LO4
Financial Statements of Limited Companies	LO1, LO5
Management Accounting: Budgeting	LO3, LO4
Management Accounting: Decision and Control	LO1, LO2, LO4, LO5

END POINT ASSESSMENT

The PDSY synoptic assessment also functions as the End Point Assessment for students studying under apprenticeships, whether for AQ2016 or Q2022.

FORMAT OF THE ASSESSMENT

The specimen synoptic assessment comprises six tasks and covers all six assessment objectives. Students will be assessed by computer-based assessment. Marking of the assessment is partially by computer and partially human marked.

In any one assessment, students may not be assessed on all content, or on the full depth or breadth of a piece of content. The content assessed may change over time to ensure validity of assessment, but all assessment criteria will be tested over time.

The following weighting is based upon the AAT Qualification Specification documentation which may be subject to variation.

	Assessment objective	Weighting
AO1	Demonstrate an understanding of the roles and responsibilities of the accounting function within an organisation and examine ways of preventing and detecting fraud and systemic weaknesses.	20%
AO2	Evaluate budgetary reporting; its effectiveness in controlling and improving organisational performance.	15%
AO3	Evaluate an organisation's accounting control systems and procedures.	15%
AO4	Analyse an organisation's decision making and control using management accounting tools.	15%
AO5	Analyse an organisation's decision making and control using ratio analysis.	20%
AO6	Analyse the internal controls of an organisation and make recommendations.	15%
	Total	100%

Time allowed: 3 hours

PASS MARK: The pass mark for all AAT assessments is 70%.

 Always keep your eye on the clock and make sure you attempt all questions!

The detailed syllabus and study guide written by the AAT can be found at:

www.aat.org.uk/

INDEX TO QUESTIONS AND ANSWERS

EXAM TECHNIQUE

- **Do not skip any of the material** in the syllabus.

- In particular, make sure you are comfortable with **assumed knowledge** from other papers at this level and those from lower levels.

- Make sure you are **familiar** with the live assessment pre-release information and have read through it at least twice.

- **Read each question** *very* carefully.

- **Double-check your answer** before committing yourself to it.

- Answer **every** question – if you do not know an answer to a multiple choice question or true/false question, you don't lose anything by guessing. Think carefully before you **guess**.

- If you are answering a multiple-choice question, **eliminate first those answers that you know are wrong.** Then choose the most appropriate answer from those that are left.

- **Don't panic** if you realise you've answered a question incorrectly. Getting one question wrong will not mean the difference between passing and failing.

Computer-based exams – tips

- Do not attempt a CBA until you have **completed all study material** relating to it.

- On the AAT website there is a CBA demonstration. It is **ESSENTIAL** that you attempt this before your real CBA. You will become familiar with how to move around the CBA screens and the way that questions are formatted, increasing your confidence and speed in the actual exam.

- Be sure you understand how to use the **software** before you start the exam. If in doubt, ask the assessment centre staff to explain it to you.

- Questions are **displayed on the screen** and answers are entered using keyboard and mouse. At the end of the exam, in the case of those units not subject to human marking, you are given a certificate showing the result you have achieved.

- In addition to the traditional multiple-choice question type, CBAs will also contain **other types of questions**, such as number entry questions, drag and drop, true/false, pick lists or drop down menus or hybrids of these.

- In some CBAs you will have to type in complete computations or written answers.

- You need to be sure you **know how to answer questions** of this type before you sit the exam, through practice.

KAPLAN'S RECOMMENDED REVISION APPROACH

QUESTION PRACTICE IS THE KEY TO SUCCESS

Success in professional examinations relies upon you acquiring a firm grasp of the required knowledge at the tuition phase. In order to be able to do the questions, knowledge is essential.

However, the difference between success and failure often hinges on your exam technique on the day and making the most of the revision phase of your studies.

The **Kaplan Study Text** is the starting point, designed to provide the underpinning knowledge to tackle all questions. However, in the revision phase, poring over text books is not the answer.

Kaplan Pocket Notes are designed to help you quickly revise a topic area; however you then need to practise questions. There is a need to progress to exam style questions as soon as possible, and to tie your exam technique and technical knowledge together.

The importance of question practice cannot be over-emphasised.

The recommended approach below is designed by expert tutors in the field, in conjunction with their knowledge of the examiner and the specimen assessment.

You need to practise as many questions as possible in the time you have left.

OUR AIM

Our aim is to get you to the stage where you can attempt exam questions confidently, to time, in a closed book environment, with no supplementary help (i.e. to simulate the real examination experience).

Practising your exam technique is also vitally important for you to assess your progress and identify areas of weakness that may need more attention in the final run up to the examination.

In order to achieve this we recognise that initially you may feel the need to practice some questions with open book help.

Good exam technique is vital.

THE KAPLAN REVISION PLAN

Stage 1: Assess areas of strengths and weaknesses

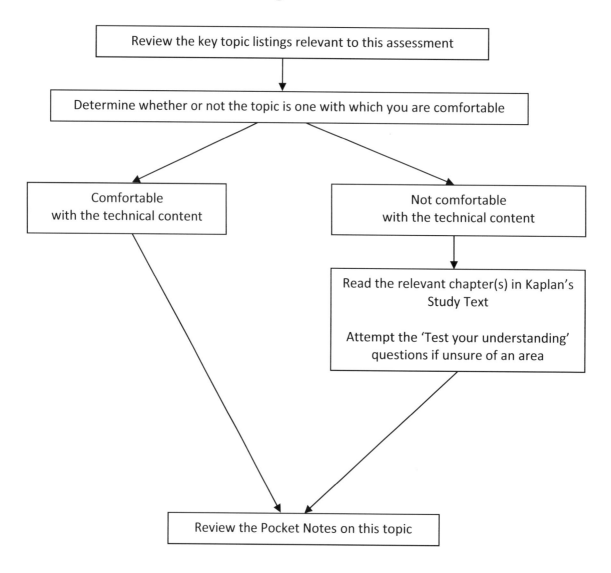

Stage 2: Familiarisation and practice questions

Follow the order of revision of topics as presented in this practice kit and attempt the questions in the order suggested.

Try to avoid referring to Study Texts and your notes and the model answer until you have completed your attempt.

Review your attempt with the model answer and assess how much of the answer you achieved.

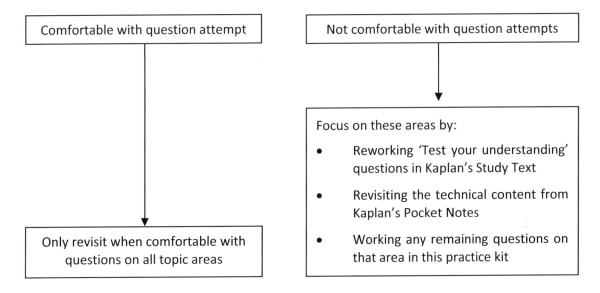

Stage 3: Final pre-exam revision

We recommend that you **attempt at least one mock examination** containing a set of previously unseen exam-standard questions based on the live assessment pre-release information.

Attempt the mock CBA online in timed, closed book conditions to simulate the real exam experience.

Also ensure that you have worked through the two sample assessments carefully and thought how to answer the same questions from the perspective of the company in the live pre-seen release.

Section 1

COMMENTARY ON LIVE PRE-RELEASE INFORMATION

1 ADVANCED PRE-RELEASE INFORMATION

INSTRUCTIONS TO CANDIDATES

This material is designed to contextualise the tasks you will receive in your live assessments.

This document has been made available to you ahead of your assessment. Studying this material will encourage you to think about the assessment topics in an integrated way, which is necessary for performing well in the synoptic assessment.

You will not be able to take a copy of this document into the assessment with you. However, you will have access to this material through pop-up windows in the assessment.

ARGENT ELECTRIC MOTORS LTD (AEM LTD)

COMPANY BACKGROUND AND HISTORY

Argent Electric Motors Ltd (AEM Ltd) sells both new and used electric cars. AEM Ltd was established three years ago and is owned by the four directors who created the company, all of whom continue to work full-time within the business and form its senior management team.

All the directors previously worked for one of the largest motor vehicle retailers in the UK and have extensive knowledge of the motor vehicle industry. They established AEM Ltd to take advantage of the increased demand for electric motor vehicles arising from both increased consumer demand for more environmentally friendly vehicles and the introduction of UK government legislation phasing out the sale of new gasoline cars.

The company operates 15 car showrooms across the UK where customers can view the different models and take advantage of the opportunity to test drive a vehicle. In addition, AEM Ltd sells cars via their website. All used cars are sold with a two-year warranty and free breakdown cover with a national motoring organisation. Customers have the option to purchase a fixed cost three-year servicing plan at a guaranteed minimum 20% discount off the standard servicing price schedule. The company also provides a price match promise for any new car purchased online.

Over the past three years AEM Ltd has grown rapidly and now has a turnover of over £40 million and employs more than 250 full-time employees.

COMPANY PHILOSOPHY

The environmental benefits of electric vehicles are at the core of the AEM Ltd brand. The reduction in emissions from electric vehicles, lower carbon footprint and noise reduction are the focus for all marketing campaigns undertaken by AEM Ltd.

Operationally, AEM Ltd also looks to minimise its impact on the environment. All showrooms are designed to reduce energy consumption and the organisations within its supply chain are assessed for their approach to sustainability before AEM Ltd works with them.

The business also understands the competitive nature of the car retailing market in the UK and through its price promise looks to provide the highest levels of value for money to its customers.

OPERATING MODEL

AEM Ltd has its head office in an industrial estate in Wembley in north west London. All the management team, finance and other central services are based at this location. The site also has a large warehouse, from which it distributes the vehicles sold online directly to customers.

Operational costs need to be kept as low as possible to allow AEM Ltd to price match against its competitors so effective inventory management is fundamental. Managers at the UK showrooms are given inventory turnover targets for used cars and a threshold is established for the total level of vehicle parts held at each location.

MARKET DEVELOPMENTS

The level of ownership of electric vehicles has dramatically increased over the three years that AEM Ltd has been operating and competition in the marketplace is increasing as a result. However, the AEM Ltd brand remains strong and is helping the business continue to grow.

To help further expand the business AEM Ltd has recently acquired Weldon Vehicles Ltd (WV Ltd). Although not noted for selling electric vehicles, WV Ltd has four showrooms in the North of England and has an excellent reputation.

AEM LTD PERFORMANCE APPRAISAL

Over the first two years the performance of the business was primarily assessed based on its financial results. The senior management team concluded that as the business was more established, a rounded approach should be taken to assessing performance, and it was decided that a balanced scorecard, analysing a wider range of areas, should be adopted.

Perspective 1 – How customers view the business

The senior management team view customer perception of the business as a fundamental element of its future success. There are two distinct elements to this: customer experience and satisfaction when acquiring a vehicle, and then the ongoing relationship with respect to servicing and support over their ownership of the vehicle.

The data shows that customer satisfaction is high when purchasing a vehicle but that the ongoing aftercare performance is disappointing.

Perspective 2 – Employee development

AEM Ltd's focus is to provide a workplace where employees develop their abilities and skills through training, and to provide a culture which encourages learning and development to take place. The car-sale industry has a reputation for low levels of staff engagement and loyalty to their employer.

Formalised induction courses have been introduced and all new staff are assigned a mentor whose role is to offer guidance and support. An extensive internal training programme has been established and staff are encouraged to contribute to the staff suggestion scheme.

Overall performance in this area has been positive, although feedback suggests that while many good features have been introduced, the culture within the business is that they are not promoted or encouraged.

Perspective 3 – Internal efficiency

Developing and maintaining internal processes is seen as crucial to the business. Functions such as vehicle deliveries, after sales service and supplier relationships need to be as efficient as possible to deliver the growth wanted by the senior management team.

Performance in this area has been strong.

Perspective 4 – Financial performance

Although there has been a good start to the business it is important that the financial fundamentals of the business remain strong.

Encouragingly, the business continues to achieve solid growth in its financial performance. However, with the recent acquisition of WV Ltd, there is some concern that the business might be developing too quickly for its capital base.

STAFF

Some of AEM Ltd's key personnel are listed below:

Chief Executive	Andrew Watts
Finance Director	Alison Clockwell
Operations Director	William Glass
Sales & Marketing Director	Barbara Sinta
Financial Controller	Chris Davies
Purchasing Manager	Graham Musa
Warehouse Manager	Susan March
Credit Controller	Ellen Peterson
Accounts Payable Clerk	Vinod Albert
Accounts Receivable Clerk	Billy Stark
General Accounts Clerk and Cashier	Katrina Walter
Payroll clerk	John Morris

ARGENT ELECTRIC MOTORS LTD FINANCIAL STATEMENTS

(Note these do not include the results of Weldon Vehicles Ltd, which was acquired in January 20X3.

Argent Electric Motors Ltd – Statement of profit or loss for the year ended 31 December 20X2

Continuing operations	£000
Revenue	40,230
Cost of sales	(28,750)
Gross profit	11,480
Operating expenses	(9,100)
Profit from operations	2,380
Finance costs	(495)
Profit before tax	1,885
Tax	(360)
Profit for the period from continuing operations	1,525

Argent Electric Motors Ltd – Statement of financial position as at 31 December 20X2

	£000
ASSETS	
Non-current assets	
Property, plant and equipment	2,170
	2,170
Current assets	
Inventories	4,885
Trade receivables	950
Cash and cash equivalents	945
	6,780
Total assets	8,950
EQUITY AND LIABILITIES	
Equity	
Ordinary share capital (£1 shares)	400
Retained earnings	2,035
Total equity	2,435
Non-current liabilities	
Bank loan	3,200
	3,200
Current liabilities	
Trade payables	2,955
Tax liabilities	360
	3,315
Total liabilities	6,515
Total equity and liabilities	8,950

2   ANALYSIS AND COMMENTARY

A key question is how best to assess the pre-release information. One approach is to read through each section and ask yourself what this is telling you about the company, potential control issues and the effectiveness of any systems and processes described. Let us take each section in turn:

COMPANY BACKGROUND AND HISTORY

Detail from pre-seen	Commentary
AEM sells both new and used electric cars	What controls are in place to ensure the quality and price when purchasing used cars? For example, is there a risk that a manager will pay a very high price to a friend?
UK government legislation	How does AEM ensure it keeps up to date with changes in legislation?
The company operates 15 car showrooms across the UK	To what extent are showroom mangers given autonomy to run their showrooms and to what extent is there centralised control through top-down budgeting and imposed targets? How much power do managers have to offer discounts to win sales and how is this controlled to stop excessive discounts being given to friends?
In addition, AEM Ltd sells cars via their website.	Are customer details, especially for debit cards and bank details, kept secure? Are there adequate controls to reduce the risk of cyber-attacks, data theft, hacking, etc? Is the company GDPR compliant?
Over the past three years AEM Ltd has grown rapidly	High growth often exposes weaknesses in control systems and the need for more robust control and IT systems. Such changes will need to be evaluated clearly, using CBA, and managed well, for example, by parallel running. In addition, high growth could result in cash flow problems and even overtrading. High growth makes incremental budgeting more difficult and is an argument for some degree of ZBB.
Employs more than 250 full-time employees	Are there sufficient checks and controls surrounding recruitment, payroll, overtime sheets, etc?

COMPANY PHILOSOPHY

Detail from pre-seen	Commentary
The environmental benefits of EVs are at the core of the AEM brand	What controls are in place to ensure marketing campaigns do not exaggerate the benefits of EVs and so risk damaging the brand?
AEM also looks to minimise its environmental impact	Are there targets to monitor this – e.g. energy usage, waste generated, etc?
Supply chain partners are assessed for sustainability	What criteria are used? Are these KPIs checked and signed off before a new supplier can be authorised?

OPERATING MODEL

Detail from pre-seen	Commentary
All the management team, finance and other central services are based at this location	What controls are in place to ensure marketing campaigns do not exaggerate the benefits of EVs and so risk damaging the brand?
The site also has a large warehouse	What controls are there over access, deliveries, sending goods out, stock takes, etc?
Operational costs need to be kept as low as possible	This will need to be reinforced by having good controls over the purchasing cycle
Effective inventory management is fundamental	Inventories presumably refer mainly to cars in showrooms but could include spare parts, oil, etc. What processes are there to sell off cars if they have been held in inventory for too long? Who takes responsibility for any losses suffered – the showroom manager or the purchasing team?
Managers at the UK showrooms are given inventory turnover targets for used cars	Doesn't sound like there is much participation. Do managers consider targets to be fair or demotivating?
A threshold is established for the total level of vehicle parts held at each location	Not told if this involves participation or if it imposed.

MARKET DEVELOPMENTS

Detail from pre-seen	Commentary
Competition in the marketplace is increasing	Are targets set for, say, market share? Are rivals monitored to assess risk from rivals?
AEM has recently acquired WV Ltd	WV may have different systems so potential risks over lack of compatibility / integration.

AEM LTD PERFORMANCE APPRAISAL

Detail from pre-seen	Commentary
Ongoing aftercare is disappointing.	High risk of damaging brand and increasing threat of losing potential customers to rivals.
Formalised induction courses have been introduced and all new staff are assigned a mentor whose role is to offer guidance and support.	Are KPIs measured for the % of staff who have undertaken induction and mentoring? What about older staff?
The culture within the business is that they are not promoted or encouraged.	Risk of losing trained and experienced staff to rivals. Are KPIs measured for staff retention / turnover?
Vehicle deliveries, after sales service and supplier relationships need to be as efficient as possible to deliver the growth wanted by the senior management team.	How are these measured / controlled – e.g. % vehicle deliveries in time slot promised, % vehicles rejected on delivery, customer satisfaction with after sales service, % of phone calls answered within 3 minutes, etc?

STAFF

Detail from pre-seen	Commentary
Separate Accounts Payable and Accounts Receivable clerks	Should enable good segregation of duties
No IT director	List is not comprehensive ("Some of AEM Ltd's key personnel are listed below") but the lack of an IT Director could be risky if integrating systems with WV Ltd and managing growth.

ARGENT ELECTRIC MOTORS LTD FINANCIAL STATEMENTS

Some form of ratio analysis will feature in task 5 in your live assessment.

It is worth calculating ratios using the information in the pre-release document to see if any key problems are highlighted:

	Working	y/e 31/12/X2
Gross margin	11,480/40,230	28.5%
Operating margin	2,380/40,230	5.9%
ROCE	2,380/(2,435 + 3,200)	42.2%
Current ratio	6,780/3,315	2.05:1
Quick ratio	(950 + 945)/3,315	0.57:1
Inventory days	(4,885/28,750) × 365	62.0 days
Receivables days	(950/40,230) × 365	8.6 days
Payables days	(2,955/28,750) × 365	37.5 days
Operating cycle	62.0 + 8.6 - 37.5	33.1 days
Gearing (Debt/Equity)	3,200/2,435	1.31:1
Gearing (debt/total long term finance)	3,200/(2,435 + 3,200)	56.8%
Interest cover	2,380/495	4.81:1

Given all this, we can make the following comments:

- We do not have comparatives in the pre-seen making it impossible to discuss movements or trends. Expect to see comparatives in the live assessment!

- Inventory will include cars to be sold, long with spare parts and consumables. Inventory days thus seem very high as it shows vehicles are owned for two months on average before being sold. Given the high growth market, one would expect this to be lower and it possibly highlights problems with purchasing second cars and/or pricing decisions.

WHAT NEXT?

You do not need to learn any of the above analysis – the aim is to help you feel comfortable with the company and what it does and to think about the assessment topics in an integrated way.

However

- You may need to refer to the financial statements in order to calculate ratios for task 5.

- Even if it appears that all relevant information is given to you within the tasks, you can still add to your answer by referring back to the pre-seen. For example,

  Better purchasing controls could help "to deliver the growth wanted by the senior management team."

  More participation over target setting to help reduce the risk of staff leaving due to a feeling that "they are not promoted or encouraged".

Section 2

PRACTICE QUESTIONS

TASK 1.1

Assessment objective 1	Demonstrate an understanding of the roles and responsibilities of the accounting function within an organisation and examine ways of preventing and detecting fraud and systemic weaknesses.

1 STATUTORY DUTY

Who has the statutory duty to prepare accounts for AEM Ltd?

The company auditors.	
The directors of the company.	
Finance Director.	
Financial Controller.	
Companies House.	

2 RESPONSIBILITY

Who is responsible for maintaining sound risk management and internal control systems within AEM Ltd?

The company auditors.	
The directors of the company.	
Finance Director.	
Financial Controller.	
Companies House.	

3   BANK RECONCILIATION 1

You are assisting with the month-end bank reconciliation at AEM Ltd.

The bank statement has been compared with the cash book and the following differences identified:

1   Cheques totalling £1,629 paid into the bank at the end of the month are not showing on the bank statement.

2   Bank interest paid of £106 was not entered in the cash book.

3   A cheque for £350 written on 2 January has been incorrectly entered in the cash book at 2 December.

4   Receipts from website customers of £1,645 had cleared the bank but have not been entered in the cash book.

The balance showing on the bank statement at 31 December is a credit of £363 and the balance in the cash book is a debit of £103.

Use the following table to show the THREE adjustments you need to make to the cash book.

Adjustment	Amount £	Debit/Credit

4   BANK RECONCILIATION 2

Which of the following errors would be picked up by a bank reconciliation? (Select all that apply)

	Yes	No
A trade customer was accidentally invoiced twice for the same item.		
A trade customer took a 2% prompt payment discount despite not having paid within the timescales required to earn a discount.		
Bank interest received had not been posted to the cash book.		
A payment to a supplier of £2,500 had accidentally been posted as £250.		

5   SALES LEDGER CONTROL ACCOUNT RECONCILIATION 1

You are working on the final accounts of a company that operates a manual accounting system.

You have the following information:

(a)   A casting error has been made and one of the customer accounts has been undercast by £65.

(b)   Sales returns totalling £280 have not been entered in a customer's individual ledger.

(c)   A receipt of £1,300 from a customer has been credited to the customer's account in the sales ledger as 130.

(d)   A credit sale of £3,000 (excluding VAT at 20%) has not been included in the relevant customer's account in the sales ledger.

(e)   A customer account with a balance of £99 has been duplicated in the list of balances.

(f)   A customer with a credit balance of £50 has been listed as a debit balance of £50.

You now need to make the appropriate adjustments in the table below.

For each adjustment clearly state the amount and whether the item should be added or subtracted from the list of balances. If no adjustment is required enter '0' into the amount column.

	Add/Subtract	£
Total from list of balances		1,100
Adjustment for (a)		
Adjustment for (b)		
Adjustment for (c)		
Adjustment for (d)		
Adjustment for (e)		
Adjustment for (f)		
Revised total to agree with SLCA		3,116

6   SALES LEDGER CONTROL ACCOUNT RECONCILIATION 2

Which of the following errors would be picked up by performing a sales ledger control account reconciliation?

	Yes	No
A trade customer was accidentally invoiced twice for the same item.		
A trade customer was sold items at the wrong price.		
Credit balances had been omitted from the list of receivables balances.		
A payment from a customer of £230 had accidentally been posted as £320 to their individual account in the receivables ledger.		

7   PURCHASES LEDGER CONTROL ACCOUNT RECONCILIATION

You are working on the final accounts of a company that operates a manual accounting system.

You have the following information:

(a)   A payment of £1,277 to a supplier has been debited to the supplier's account in the purchases ledger as £1,722.

(b)   A supplier with a debit balance of £2,170 has been listed as a credit balance.

(c)   A credit purchase return of £1,000 (net of VAT at 20%) has not been included in the relevant supplier's account in the purchase ledger.

(d)   A casting error has been made and one of the supplier accounts has been overcast by £132.

(e)   A supplier account with a balance of £2,100 has been omitted from the list.

(f)   A credit purchase has been entered into the individual account net of VAT at 20%. The net amount is £600.

You now need to make the appropriate adjustments in the table below. For each adjustment clearly state the amount and whether the item should be added or subtracted from the list of balances.

	Add/Subtract	£
Total from list of balances		132,589
Adjustment for (a)		
Adjustment for (b)		
Adjustment for (c)		
Adjustment for (d)		
Adjustment for (e)		
Adjustment for (f)		
Revised total to agree with PLCA		129,582

8   ERRORS

You are working on the accounting records of AEM Ltd.

A trial balance has been drawn up and a suspense account opened. You need to make some corrections and adjustments for the year ended 31 December 20X2.

You may ignore VAT in this task.

Record the journal entries needed in the general ledger to deal with the items below.

(a)   Motor expenses of £4,500 have been posted to the Motor Vehicles at Cost account in error. The other side of the entry is correct.

Journal

	Dr £	Cr £

(b)   Office sundries costing £16 were paid for by cash. Only the entry to the cash account was made.

Journal

	Dr £	Cr £

(c) No entries have been made for closing inventory of spare parts as at 31 December 20X2. It has been valued at a selling price of £50,400. The sales price has had 20% added onto its original cost.

Journal

	Dr £	Cr £

(d) Discounts allowed of £1,270 have been posted as £1,720 on both sides of the entry.

Journal

	Dr £	Cr £

9 CHANGEOVER

The Board of AEM Ltd are considering updating the accounting system.

Alison Clockwell (FD) is suggesting that the direct changeover method be adopted. However, Andrew Watts (CEO) has argued that direct changeover is usually the highest risk alternative available.

Which TWO of the following controls can mitigate the risk of system failure during direct changeover?

Testing	
Training	
System documentation	
Data backup	
Check digits	

10   INFORMATION SYSTEM CONTROLS

Information system controls can be classified as 'security controls' and 'integrity controls'.

Drag and drop the following controls into the correct category.

	Security	Integrity
Locked doors		
Passwords		
Batch totals		
Reconciliation		
CCTV		
Check digits		
Authorisation of data entry		
Fire alarms		

11   PURCHASE CYCLE CONTROLS 1

AEM Ltd has experienced occasions when payment was made for goods not received.

Which TWO of the following controls in a purchase cycle could be implemented to reduce the risk of payment of goods not received?

Sequentially pre-numbered purchase requisitions and sequence check.	
Matching of goods received note with purchase invoice.	
Goods are inspected for condition and quantity and agreed to purchase order before acceptance.	
Daily update of inventory system.	

12   PURCHASE CYCLE CONTROLS 2

AEM Ltd has experienced occasions when unnecessary goods and services were purchased.

Which TWO of the following controls in the purchase cycle could be implemented to reduce the risk of procurement of unnecessary goods and services?

Centralised purchasing department.	
Sequentially pre-numbered purchase requisitions and sequence check.	
Orders can only be placed with suppliers from the approved suppliers list.	
All purchase requisitions are signed as authorised by an appropriate manager.	

13 EXPENSE CLAIM CONTROLS

Harry Grisham has been appointed as the new IT manager at AEM Ltd. Harry really enjoys the job and even though the remuneration is not great, the other managers at the company have explained the way they 'get around' that issue. The sales manager explains to Harry that the key is to 'put everything on expenses – private petrol, drinks and even clothing. It's all fine and as long as you have a receipt, no-one in the finance department will question it'. He continues that 'It's fine because the board are aware of it and turn a blind eye'.

Which ONE of the following essential internal control measures is evidently missing?

AEM Ltd lacks a control environment as the board are not setting an ethical tone at the top.	
AEM Ltd lacks an Internal Audit department.	
AEM Ltd lacks an experienced finance manager.	
AEM Ltd lacks an external auditor.	

14 PASSWORDS 1

You have been asked to set up a password for WV Ltd.'s accounting system.

Which of the following would be the most secure?

24june1963	
LaraJo	
mypassword	
Qwerty123!#	

15 PASSWORDS 2

You have been asked to set up a new system of passwords for AEM Ltd.'s accounting system.

Which TWO of the following would reduce the effectiveness of passwords?

Requirement that passwords are changed every two weeks	
Users are allowed to choose their own passwords	
Automatic lock-out after 3 failed attempts to access system	
Making the sharing of passwords a disciplinary offence	
Displaying the password on the screen when entered	

16 INTERNAL CONTROLS 1

An internal control system in an organisation consists of five components: the control environment, the risk assessment process, the information system, control activities and monitoring of controls.

Match each of the following activities to the component that it illustrates.

	Control environment	Information system	Control activities
The process of preparing the financial statements			
Locking the inventory storeroom			

17 INTERNAL CONTROLS 2

WV Ltd is looking at introducing new internal controls to help reduce the risk of fraud.

Match each of the following activities to the type of control that it illustrates.

	Authorisation	Information processing	Physical control
The financial controller will count petty cash on a weekly basis			
There will be two keys to a locked safe: one held by the FD and the other by the CEO.			

18 INTERNAL CONTROLS 3

AEM Ltd is looking at introducing new computer controls to reduce payroll fraud. Computer controls can be described as "general" and "application".

Match each of the following activities to the type of computer control that it illustrates.

	General	Application
Storing extra copies of programs and data files off-site		
New programmes to check data fields on input transactions		
Manual checks to ensure that input data were authorised		
Password protection limiting access to data		
Range checks on payroll processing		
Manual checks to ensure that timesheets are authorised before details are processed		

19   INTERNAL CONTROLS 4

AEM Ltd is looking at introducing new internal controls but the directors are concerned that even the best controls still have limitations.

Indicate whether the following limitations are true or false.

	True	False
The cost of implementing controls may be more expensive than the benefits gained due to reduced risk		
The effectiveness of many controls rely on the integrity of those applying them		
Internal controls are only applied to material items so smaller items remain unchecked		
Standard controls may not be designed to deal with unusual transactions		

20   FRAUD 1

The financial controller is concerned that some showroom staff may misappropriate customer remittances for small items, such as spare parts, that customers may buy.

Which TWO of the following control activities would best reduce the risk of this fraud occurring?

Segregation of duties between cash payments and recording at head office	
Post opening by two people	
Daily reconciliation of recorded till sales and cash taken in the showroom	
Regular banking of cash and cheques received in the showroom	

21   FRAUD 2

The financial controller is worried that fictitious employees could be included on the payroll by a dishonest employee from the accounts department.

Which ONE of the following control activities would best prevent this occurring?

Payroll standing data periodically printed out and checked on a line-by-line basis to independently held employee details	
Use of hierarchical passwords over standing data files	
Pre-authorisation of all amendments to payroll standing data by an independent official	
Supervision of the wages pay out by an independent official	

TASK 1.2

Assessment objective 2	Evaluate budgetary reporting; its effectiveness in controlling and improving organisational performance.

22 TRAINING COSTS

Staff training within AEM Ltd has lacked focus but to facilitate future expansion, the directors want formalised training schemes in place on topics such as GDPR regulations and customer service. Given this, they have appointed a new training manager, Petr Higgs.

One month later, Petr received the following email from Lauren Bristow (HR manager)

To:	Petr Higgs, Training Manager
From:	Lauren Bristow
Subject:	Costs out of control

I am writing to express concern over the results of your first month in charge of training.

In particular, you need to explain the reasons for your cost overrun:

	Budget	**Actual**
Number of trainees	20	25
Fixed costs (£)	13,000	12,900
Variable costs (£)	1,000	1,200
Total cost (£)	14,000	14,100

Adverse variance £100

Please come and see me immediately.

Petr was alarmed by the email as he didn't even know there was going to be a performance appraisal of this kind and certainly hadn't been involved in any budgeting or target setting.

He was also concerned that there seemed to be no mention of how good the training was.

(a) **BRIEFLY discuss THREE weaknesses in the above use of performance reports to improve the focus of training within AEM Ltd.**   **(9 marks)**

Weakness 1

Weakness 2

Weakness 3

(b)   Outline THREE performance indicators that could be used to assess the quality of the training provided.   **(6 marks)**

Performance Indicator 1

Performance Indicator 2

Performance Indicator 3

(Total 15 marks)

23 BUDGETING

William Glass (Operations Director) has presented a budget proposal for 20X3 for AEM Ltd for approval by the Board. Alison Clockwell (Finance Director) has already completed some analysis of the budget but is currently ill, so you have been asked to comment on the proposal.

Budget:

	Actual 20X2	Budget 20X3	% change
	£000	£000	
Sales revenue	40,230	49,322	22.6%
Cost of sales	(28,750)	(33,666)	17.1%
Gross profit	**11,480**	**15,656**	
Operating expenses	(9,100)	(10,830)	(19.0%)
Operating profit	**2,380**	**4,826**	

Analysis / assumptions:

	Actual 20X2	Budget 20X3	% change
Number of showrooms	15	21	40.0%
Number of cars sold	2,200	2,975	35.2%
Average selling price per car	£17,800	£16,447	(7.6%)
Gross profit margin	28.5%	31.7%	

Notes:

- The 20X3 budget incorporates results for WV Ltd. The actual results for 20X2 only include AEM Ltd and not WV Ltd.

- WV Ltd focusses exclusively on selling second hand cars, whereas AEM Ltd sells both new and used cars.

- AEM Ltd won an industry award for 'Customer Satisfaction" in September 20X2

- Latest market forecasts for 20X3 show a 20% growth in demand for electric vehicles, despite a predicted economic downturn.

Evaluate the budget for 20X3 by discussing the following assumed (or implied) growth rates. In your answer discuss whether or not you feel the figures are realistic and why.

(15 marks)

Figure	Whether or not realistic	Marks
Sales volume growth of 35.2%		5
Sales revenue growth of 22.6%		3
Cost of sales growth of 17.1%		3
Growth in operating expenses of 19.0%		2

Conclusion – whether or not the budget is realistic (2 marks)

24 AEM LTD'S BUDGETING PROCESS

AEM Ltd is about to undertake the next annual budgeting cycle and the Board have decided to allow more participation from managers in budget setting. All the managers involved have been provided with guidance notes to help them with the budgeting exercise.

AEM Ltd Budgeting Guidance (extracts)

Inflation:

Inflation should be allowed for when appropriate. For wages and product based costs inflation, managers can select between the RPI (retail price index) and the CPI (consumer price index which excludes mortgage payments). Both these indexes measure past inflation in the United Kingdom where AEM Ltd is based.

Note: No guidance is given about inflation of other costs.

Marketing:

The overall marketing budget is set by head office without consultation with showroom managers. AEM Ltd has marketing managers who have responsibility for different channels – for example, Gill Evans looks at traditional advertising through local newspapers, whereas Jenni Black is responsible for online marketing through the website and social media.

Each year the total marketing budget is set, taking account of desire for growth and any planned new showrooms. No account is taken of the previous year's spend. However, it is up the marketing managers to then estimate what effect this marketing spend might have on their areas of interest.

The marketing department provide sales trend analysis based on regression analysis, which produces a straight-line relationship between the marketing spend and sales volumes for previous periods.

Provide a 'SWOT' analysis of the above budget process and recommend, where appropriate changes to this process. **(15 marks)**

Note:

A 'strength' is where you feel the process is good and a 'weakness' is where you feel the process is not so good. An 'opportunity' to improve the process may exist in places and a 'threat' is best written as a bad consequence of a poor budget process.

Strengths

Weaknesses

Opportunities

Threats

TASK 1.3

Assessment objective 3	Evaluate an organisation's accounting control systems and procedures.

Note: in the sample and practice assessments task 1.3 only asked for weaknesses and explanations of implications. In this section, we have also asked for recommendations as this is useful practice for task 1.6.

25   WV LTD'S PURCHASING SYSTEM

Below is a description of the purchasing and payments system for Weldon Vehicles Ltd in respect of buying spare parts and other consumables.

Ordering

Whenever new items are required, the relevant showroom manager sends a requisition form to the ordering department. An order clerk raises a purchase order and contacts a number of suppliers to see which can despatch the goods first. This supplier is then chosen. The order clerk sends out the purchase order. This is not sequentially numbered and only orders above £100 require authorisation.

Bookkeeping

Purchase invoices are input daily by the purchase ledger clerk, Neil, who has been in the role for many years and, as an experienced team member, he does not apply any application controls over the input process. Every week the purchase day book automatically updates the purchase ledger, the purchase ledger is then posted manually to the general ledger by the purchase ledger clerk.

Payments

Weldon Vehicles Ltd maintains a current account and a number of saving (deposit) accounts. The current account is reconciled weekly but the saving (deposit) accounts are only reconciled every two months.

In order to maximise their cash and bank balance, Weldon Vehicles Ltd has recently started delaying payments to all suppliers for as long as possible. Suppliers are paid by a bank transfer. The finance director, Chloe, is given the total amount of the payments list, which she authorises and then processes the bank payments.

Required:

Identify and explain FOUR deficiencies in the system, explain the possible implication of each deficiency and provide a recommendation to address each deficiency.   (15 marks)

Weakness	Implication	Recommendation

26 WV LTD'S CASH RECEIPTS AND PAYMENTS PROCESSES

In order to support the integration of Weldon Vehicles Ltd into the business, you have been asked to review Weldon Vehicles' processes for cash receipts and payments within showrooms.

Each of Weldon Vehicles' showrooms has three cash tills (cash registers) to take payments from customers. Customers can pay for cars, parts or servicing using either cash, a debit card or a credit card. For all transactions either the card machine printouts or cash are placed in the till by the employee operating the till. To speed up the payment process, showrooms have a specific log on code which can be used to access all tills and is changed every two weeks.

At the end of the day, the tills are closed down by the showroom manager who counts the total cash in all three tills and the sum of the card machine print outs and these totals were then reconciled with the aggregated daily readings of sales taken from each till. Any discrepancies were noted on the daily sales sheet. The daily sales sheet records the sales per the tills, the cash counted and the total card machine printouts as well as any discrepancies. These sheets are scanned and emailed to the General Accounts Clerk, Maisie Fox, at the end of each week.

While most customers pay using a debit card when buying a car, approximately 30% of customers use cash for consumables, parts and servicing. Some customers still prefer to buy used cars using cash. Cash is stored in the safe at the showroom on a daily basis after the sales reconciliation has been undertaken. The safe can only be accessed via a key which the showroom manager has responsibility for. The key is stored in a drawer of the manager's desk when not being used.

Cash is transferred to the bank via daily collection by a security company. The security company provides a receipt for the sums collected, and these receipts are immediately forwarded to the General Accounts Clerk, Maisie Fox. The credit card company remits the amounts due directly into Weldon Vehicles Ltd's bank account within two days of the transaction. Debit card payments typically appear in Weldon Vehicles Ltd's bank account the same day.

On receipt of the daily sales sheets and security company receipts, the General Accounts Clerk, Maisie Fox, agrees the cash transferred by the security company has been banked and matches the cash per the daily sales sheets to bank deposit slips and to the bank statements. She then updates the cash book with the cash banked and details of the card machine printouts from the daily sales sheets. On a monthly basis, the credit card company sends a statement of all credit card receipts which Maisie filed.

Every two months, Masie reconciles the bank statements to the cash book. The reconciliations are reviewed by the Finance Director, Malik Kain who evidences his review by signature and these are filed in the accounts department. All purchases are paid by bank transfer. At the relevant payment dates, the Finance Director, Malik Kain, is given the total amount of the payments list which he authorises.

Required:

Identify and explain FIVE DEFICIENCIES in Weldon Vehicles Ltd's cash receipts and payments system and provide a recommendation to address each of these deficiencies.

(15 marks)

Control deficiency	Recommendation

27   AEM LTD'S INVENTORY COUNTING PROCESSES

Each winter, AEM Ltd is obliged to count its inventory in its warehouse and showrooms.

This year AEM Ltd arranged for an external auditor to attend some of the inventory count in the warehouse and feedback their findings. It was hoped that this would lead to improved procedures in the future. To help finish the count on time, the auditor acted as a counter and an auditor at the same time.

In the warehouse, pre-printed inventory sheets were produced which showed the designated location of all vehicles, spare parts and consumable lines and the staff were instructed to verify vehicles existed and record the number of spare parts and consumables items that they found in each location.

The warehouse was split into 8 zones with two teams being responsible for 3 zones each and then, depending on how fast each team counted the other two zones could be dealt with.

Suppliers were requested not to deliver during the warehouse counts. This policy was mostly followed but one supplier of tyres failed to obey and a large delivery was made. The driver offloaded the stock in the car park and left so as not to interfere with the counting process.

During the count, large boxes of spare air filters not yet unpacked were not opened but the slips on the side of the boxes were used to note the contents on the inventory sheets.

A note was made of damaged items but, since the Financial Controller had already done a slow-moving inventory calculation, old inventory was not recorded.

Outline 5 weaknesses and their effect on the accounting systems in the boxes below:
(15 marks)

Weakness		Effect of Weakness

Weakness	Effect of Weakness

TASK 1.4

Assessment objective 4	Analyse an organisation's decision making and control using management accounting tools.

28 STOCKING DECISIONS

As well as selling cars, WV Ltd also has an extensive servicing and repair operation at each of it showrooms. Each showroom has a storage area for holding inventory of spare parts and consumables, such as oil and air filters. WV Ltd leases all of its showrooms.

A problem facing the business is that Michelle Kahn, the owner of one of the showroom sites and premises, has informed them that she needs to undertake some building work for the next month, meaning that WV Ltd's available space will be severely limited for that period. The Directors of AEM are considering alternative sources of storage but, in the meantime, have called a meeting to discuss how best to use the limited space.

To help illustrate ideas, the following table a been produced that shows the sales and profitability of four air filters for a typical month.

Sales and profitability data

Filter type	A	B	C	D
Potential sales demand	25	30	20	40
	£	£	£	£
Selling price	15.00	12.00	12.50	10.00
Variable costs	10.00	8.00	7.00	5.00
Contribution per pack	**5.00**	**4.00**	**5.50**	**5.00**
Total contribution	125	120	110	200
Apportioned fixed overheads	(50)	(60)	(40)	(80)
Operating profit	**70**	**60**	**70**	**120**
Space required per box (square metres)	0.100	0.096	0.120	0.110
Contribution per square metre	**50**	**42**	**46**	**45**

Notes:

1   Corporate customer discounts have been excluded from the above selling prices.

2   Fixed overheads relate to showroom labour, rent and energy costs. These are apportioned on a budgeted unit basis to assist decision making.

Directors' discussion

At the Board meeting, the directors gave their views as to which of the four filter options should be made if storage space were limited.

Andrew Watts, the Chief Executive, argued that, based on total operating profits, Filter D should be stocked. His argument was that the apportioned fixed overhead had to be taken into account as it had to be covered somewhere in the business.

Barbara Sinta the Sales & Marketing Director, disagreed. Her opinion was that the allocated fixed costs were irrelevant and that they should just look at the contribution, although she was unclear whether it was better to look at contribution per filter (and pick C) or total contribution (and pick D).

Alison Clockwell, the Finance Director, thought the correct approach was to look at the contribution per square metre of space as they had limited storage, rather than the total or unit contribution. She thus favoured pack A.

(a) **BRIEFLY discuss the validity of each of the three directors' views on how the final decision should be made as to which filter option to prioritise.** **(9 marks)**

Chief Executive

Sales & Marketing Director

Finance Director

(b) BRIEFLY explain TWO other factors should be taken into consideration before making a final decision. **(6 marks)**

Factor 1

Factor 2

29 CLOSURE OF SHOWROOM

Having acquired WV Ltd at the start of 20X3, the board of AEM Ltd is now considering whether any showrooms should be closed. William Glass (Operations Director) has suggested that, given one of the WV Ltd showroom is only 3 miles from an existing AEM Ltd showroom, cost savings could be made by closing one of them without too much impact on sales. The decision is to be based on a range of factors, both financial and non-financial.

You have identified the following information for 20X3:

	Notes	Existing AEM showroom #12	Existing WV showroom #3
Revenue (£000)		2,400	2,250
Typical mark-up on purchase cost		60%	50%
% of sales likely to be lost if closed		20%	30%
Closure costs re the premises (£000)	1	70	60
Labour costs (£000)	2	75	65
Overheads saved (£000)	3	125	122

Notes:

1. Closure costs include disposals of fixtures and fittings, penalty charges for cancelling leases and costs to restore the sites to the standard required under clauses in the lease.

2.   Labour costs include the full wages for staff in each location. It can be assumed that 80% of staff will be made redundant and 20% will move to the other showroom concerned.

3.   Overheads include head office recharges of £10,000 for AEM showroom #12, and £8,000 for WV showroom #2.

(a)   Assess the decision using the relevant cash flows for 20X3 and comment on your results.   (9 marks)

(b)   Briefly explain three other factors that need to be considered.   (6 marks)

Factor 1
Factor 2
Factor 3

30   AEM LTD PLANNING

The sales of one of one of AEM's most popular electric small cars, the Ford HX6, has been in steady decline and questions are being raised about its long-term future and whether it should be dropped from the range. Directors' views are mixed as the car won many industry awards when it was first released to the market five years ago.

The HX6 is priced at £25,000 and AEM Ltd makes a contribution margin on sales of 60% on this product. This margin only accounts for variable costs. If fixed costs are averaged over all products than this product's share would be £250,000 a quarter. It is not thought that there is any directly attributable fixed cost.

The reason for the decline is thought to be because new models are available that have more features, greater range and are more energy efficient. As a result, the HX6 is no longer seen as innovative and customers feel the price is too high. To help assess the decision to discontinue the model, data has been gathered by the sales team on the volume of sales over the past two years split by quarters and your help is being requested to provide interpretation of that data.

The data analysis was performed using regression techniques where:

$$Y = a + bX$$

Y is the sales volume and X is the relevant quarter number

The data started with the quarter ended 30 Sept X1 (X = 1) and provided six quarters of data (up to X = 6). The 'b' value was found to be −2 and the 'a' value was 35 units

(a)   Using the data above complete the following table: **(6 marks)**

Quarter Number (X)	Quarter ended	Cars sold (Y)	Revenue £000	Variable Cost £000	Contribution £000
1	30/9/X1	35	875	350	525
2	31/12/X1	29	725	290	435
3	31/3/X2	27	675	270	450
4	30/6/X2	26	650	260	390
5	30/9/X2	24	600	240	360
6	31/12/X2	24	600	240	360
7	31/3/X3				
8	30/6/X3				
9	30/9/X3				
10	31/12/X3				

(b)   Briefly discuss the meaning of the value 'b' above and your findings using the data and comment on whether AEM Ltd, from a financial viewpoint, would want to continue to offer this model up to and including quarter to 31/10/X3.

(7 marks)

(c)   Briefly discuss any non-financial considerations regarding the withdrawal of a particular model from sale.   **(2 marks)**

TASK 1.5

Assessment objective 5	Analyse an organisation's decision making and control using ratio analysis.

31   OVERTRADING

Despite the company having significant cash reserves, Andrew Watts has expressed concerns that AEM Ltd's high forecast growth rates may result in an overtrading position, where financial and other resources are insufficient for the rate of expansion.

To help assess the extent of this risk a range of ratios have been calculated to create a scorecard based on AEM Ltd's forecast performance for y/e 31 December 20X3. This scorecard excludes WV Ltd to improve comparability. These are given below, together with some ratios from y/e 31 December 20X2.

(a)   Complete the scorecard by calculating the missing ratios.   (10 marks)

AEM Ltd (excluding WV Ltd) Scorecard	X3	X2
Profitability and gearing		
Gross profit %	27.5%	28.5%
Operating profit %	6.6%	%
Return on capital employed	38.8%	%
Gearing (debt/equity)	1.62×	1.31×
Liquidity ratios		
Current ratio	3.28:1	2.05:1
Acid test/Quick ratio	1.26:1	:1
Working capital days		
Inventory holding period	64 days	days
Trade receivables collection period	12 days	9 days
Trade payables payment period	32 days	38 days
Working capital operating cycle	44 days	days

(b)   Select the ONE correct observation about each aspect of business performance below.   (10 marks)

Profitability

20X3 will be a year of steady, if unspectacular, progress. Although margins have dipped, the return on capital employed has been kept constant.	
The changes in gross margin could be due to cost control problems concerning head office costs.	
Increased competition and the resulting pressure on prices could explain the change in each of the three profitability ratios.	

Gearing

The increased gearing ratio proves that the company has no problems raising additional debt finance.	
It is likely that the interest cover ratio has increased.	
The increased gearing ratio shows that the shareholders' position has become more risky.	

Liquidity

Both ratios have increased, which indicates that the company is less solvent.	
A higher quick ratio is a clear indicator of overtrading.	
The change in both the current and quick ratios could be partly explained by the increase in the receivables period.	

Working capital

The working capital cycle has worsened. This increases the possibility of AEM overtrading.	
There is a welcome improvement in the working capital cycle, mainly due to the change in the payment period for payables.	
The working capital cycle is worse than a year ago, solely because of the change in inventory days.	

Overall performance

Despite overall growth, AEM is expected to have a difficult year in 20X3 and needs to investigate why key ratios will be deteriorating.	
20X3 looks to be a disaster for AEM.	
There is no evidence of possible control problems.	

32   ANALYSIS OF WV LTD

Alison Clockwell, the Finance Director, is preparing a presentation for the board of directors to discuss possible control problems within the business, with particular emphasis on developing best practice for both AEM Ltd and WV Ltd. She has asked you to complete a comparative 'score card' of key financial ratios comparing AEM Ltd and WV Ltd, which she will use as part of her presentation.

Extracts from accounts of WV Ltd	20X2
	£000
Profitability	
Sales revenue	13,945
Cost of sales	7,070
Profit from operations	1,325
Assets	
Non-current assets	3,559
Inventories	1,162
Trade receivables	1,233
Total	**5,954**
Equities and liabilities	
Equity	3,958
Non-current liabilities – loans	792
Trade payables	581
Bank overdraft	423
Tax liabilities	200
Total	**5,954**

(a)   Complete the scorecard by calculating the missing ratios.   (10 marks)

20X2	AEM	WV
Profitability		
Gross profit %	28.5%	
Operating profit %	5.9%	9.5%
Return on capital employed	42.2%	
Liquidity ratios		
Current ratio	2.1:1	
Acid test/Quick ratio	0.6:1	0.6:1
Working capital days		
Inventory holding period	62 days	60 days
Trade receivables collection period	9 days	12 days
Trade payables payment period	38 days	
Working capital cycle	33 days	

(b)   Assess the following statements and indicate whether they are true or false.

(10 marks)

Statement	True	False
The difference in gross margins could be explained by WV Ltd offering a 50% discount on servicing for two years on all cars sold.		
If AEM Ltd has delayed paying suppliers at the year end, then this would contribute to the difference in current ratios.		
The difference in the ROCE figures could be explained by the fact that WV Ltd is much older than AEM Ltd.		
A warehouse employee in AEM Ltd was found to have stolen spare parts and given them to friends. This would contribute to the difference in the ROCE figures.		
Inadequate controls over expense claims for managers within TW Ltd could contribute to the difference in the operating margins figures.		

33 CASH AND PROFIT

The directors of AEM Ltd have been having a discussion on the financial ratios of the business and which should take priority for the business.

Andrew Watts (CEO) stated "All that seems to matter is profit and profit-based ratios. Every time I watch a business program on television, profit is pretty much the first thing that is talked about." It is for this reason that I have instructed the accounts department to delay the payment of our next rent bills for the warehouse. This should increase our profitability at a vital time as I am meeting a team of venture capitalists soon to discuss future funding.

Barbara Sinta (Sales & Marketing Director) in part agreed but added "I feel that cash flow and liquidity ratios are also vital. Surely the venture capitalists would be interested in how much cash we generate as well? However, at the end of the day cash and profit seem to be the same thing. I spend money on spare parts or wages and the same figure ends up in the profit and loss account, so if we are profitable we must have more cash coming in that going out."

Alison Clockwell (Finance Director) is a little despairing of her friends and colleagues and has asked you summarise the issue of 'profits versus cash' for her to use at the next board meeting where she will attempt to explain.

Briefly explain the profits and cash issues mentioned above under the following headings:

Why is profit important in business? (5 marks)
Why must cash also be considered in business? (5 marks)

Does the cash equal the profit?	(5 marks)
Discuss whether delaying the rent payment will be effective in increasing profits and the ethical stance the accounting department should take to the request. (5 marks)	

TASK 1.6

Assessment objective 6	Analyse the internal controls of an organisation and make recommendations.

34   WELDON VEHICLES LTD'S PAYROLL SYSTEMS

You have been asked to review the payroll systems of Weldon Vehicles Ltd (WV Ltd).

As WV Ltd is a small company it has not always been considered necessary to issue a contract of employment to every new member of staff, especially for some warehouse staff who want to work part time or for a limited period. Instead, a new starter in the warehouse may be told verbally what their hours of work and rate of pay will be along with other key terms and conditions.

At the start of a shift, each warehouse employee uses a clock card to record their time of arrival. They use the same machine to clock out at the end of their shift. The clock machine is in a quiet corner of each warehouse to avoid disruption. The clocking in and out process is not supervised. The rack where the clock cards are kept always contains one or two spare cards in case any get spoiled or damaged by the machine. Once an employee has clocked in, they are entitled to sit and have a drink and something to eat before starting work. At the end of each week, the warehouse manager collects the clock cards from the rack in each cafe and posts them to the home of the Payroll Manager.

Many administrative staff now work from home and some can claim overtime if their hours exceed their contracted standard hours each week. Given staff do not have to come into the office, their record their start and end times, and daily hours on a shared google sheet. These figures are then used by the payroll manager to determine any overtime payments.

Identify and explain FIVE DEFICIENCIES in WV Ltd's payroll system, and provide a recommendation to address each of these deficiencies. (15 marks)

Deficiency	Recommendation

35 DALE HOME CHARGING LTD'S SALES AND DESPATCH SYSTEM

The Board of AEM Ltd are considering buying Dale Home Charging Ltd ('Dale'), a company that sells and installs home charging points for electric vehicles. As well as selling smaller domestic charging units that customers can install themselves, with the help of a qualified electrician, Dale also offers larger charging stations that can be designed and fitted to the customers' individual specification. The company trades both B2C and B2B with business customers typically more interested in the charging station installation, whereas individuals are more likely to buy the smaller domestic units. Dale also sells spare and replacement parts for all charging units. Dale has a dedicated sales team to manage the relationship with larger firms but orders from smaller organisations and the public are mainly placed through the company's website, while some are also made via telephone.

William Glass (Operations Director) has started to investigate the company in more detail and has some concerns over its sales and despatch system. He is reasonably happy over the way larger firms are dealt with but has concerns over telephone and website transactions.

Online orders are automatically checked against inventory records and installation booking schedules for availability; telephone orders, however, are checked manually by order clerks after the call. A follow-up call is usually made to customers if there is insufficient inventory or problems meeting specified installation dates. When taking telephone orders, clerks note down the details on plain paper and afterwards they complete a three-part pre-printed order form. These order forms are not sequentially numbered and are sent manually to both despatch and the accounts department.

As the company is expanding, business customers are able to place online orders which will exceed their agreed credit limit by 10%. Online orders are automatically forwarded to the despatch and accounts department.

For parts and smaller charging units, a daily pick list is printed by the despatch department and this is used by the warehouse team to despatch goods. The goods are accompanied by a despatch note and all customers are required to sign a copy of this. On return, the signed despatch notes are given to the warehouse team to file.

The sales quantities are entered from the despatch notes and the authorised sales prices are generated by the invoicing system. If a discount has been given, say for a large order, then this has to be manually entered by the sales clerk onto the invoice.

Due to the expansion of the company, and as there is a large number of sale invoices, extra accounts staff have been asked to help out temporarily with producing the sales invoices. Normally it is only two sales clerks who produce the sales invoices.

Identify and explain FIVE deficiencies in Dale's sales and despatch system and provide a recommendation to address each of these deficiencies. **(15 marks)**

Deficiency	Recommendation

Deficiency	Recommendation

36 NEW HUMAN RESOURCES SOFTWARE SYSTEM

At the recent Board meeting, the Directors of AEM Ltd discussed the balanced scorecard approach to performance management and how it could be improved. Andrew Watts (Chief Executive) felt that AEM needed a more structured way of addressing any issues that had arisen. In particular, he was concerned that many employees felt that they were not encouraged within their roles or had little expectation of promotion.

William Glass (Operations Director) agreed and argued that staff needed more detailed and fair job gradings, and that the company should introduce a comprehensive set of KPIs for staff. This would make smaller, more incremental promotions more feasible and enable frequent feedback and performance appraisal. Furthermore, he reported that he had been in discussions with a software vendor to provide a package, 'Workweek', that should enable this and provide greater consistency and a more robust structure to recruitment, expense claims and other HR functions.

You have been asked to appraise the proposed new system over a three year planning horizon and have determined the following:

- AEM will need to spend £24,000 upgrading computer hardware. This will have a useful life of 3 years before being scrapped for zero net proceeds. Annual depreciation will thus be £8,000 per annum.

- The cost of the 'Workweek' software will be an upfront £20,000, together with an annual fee of £4,000.

- Initial training costs of £30,000 will be required

- Incremental costs of performance appraisals, setting up and reviewing KPIs, and job grading are anticipated to be £16,000 per annum.

(a) **Evaluate the financial implications of introducing the new system using discounted cash flows and the following template, and comment on your answer.** (9 marks)

	Time 0	Year 1	Year 2	Year 3
Hardware				
Software				
Training				
Other costs				
Net cash flow				
Discount factor @ 10%	1	0.909	0.826	0.753
Present value				
Net Present Value				
Comment:				

(b)   As part of a wider cost-benefit analysis ('CBA'), explain THREE benefits of the new system not covered in part (a), including how these factors might be quantified and incorporated into the CBA.   **(6 marks)**

Benefit 1	
Benefit 2	
Benefit 3	

Section 3

ANSWERS TO PRACTICE QUESTIONS

TASK 1.1

Assessment objective 1	Demonstrate an understanding of the roles and responsibilities of the accounting function within an organisation and examine ways of preventing and detecting fraud and systemic weaknesses.

1 STATUTORY DUTY

Who has the statutory duty to prepare accounts for AEM Ltd?

The company auditors.	
The directors of the company.	✓
Finance Director.	
Financial Controller.	
Companies House.	

2 RESPONSIBILITY

Who is responsible for maintaining sound risk management and internal control systems within AEM Ltd?

The company auditors.	
The directors of the company.	✓
Finance Director.	
Financial Controller.	
Companies House.	

3 BANK RECONCILIATION 1

Adjustment	Amount £	Debit/Credit
Adjustment for (2)	106	Cr
Adjustment for (3)	350	Dr
Adjustment for (4)	1,645	Dr

Note:

Reconciliation

Cash book

Balance b/d	103	ADJUSTMENT (2)	106
ADJUSTMENT (3)	350		
ADJUSTMENT (4)	1,645		
		Balance c/d	1,992
	2,098		2,098

Balance of bank account	363
Uncleared lodgements	1,629
	1,992

4 BANK RECONCILIATION 2

	Yes	No
A trade customer was accidentally invoiced twice for the same item.		✓
A trade customer took a 2% prompt payment discount despite not having paid within the timescales required to earn a discount.		✓
Bank interest received had not been posted to the cash book.	✓	
A payment to a supplier of £2,500 had accidentally been posted as £250.	✓	

5 SALES LEDGER CONTROL ACCOUNT RECONCILIATION 1

	Add/Subtract	£
Total from list of balances		1,100
Adjustment for (a)	Add	65
Adjustment for (b)	Subtract	280
Adjustment for (c)	Subtract	1,170
Adjustment for (d)	Add	3,600
Adjustment for (e)	Subtract	99
Adjustment for (f)	Subtract	100
Revised total to agree with SLCA		3,116

6 **SALES LEDGER CONTROL ACCOUNT RECONCILIATION 2**

	Yes	No
A trade customer was accidentally invoiced twice for the same item.		✓
A trade customer was sold items at the wrong price.		✓
Credit balances had been omitted from the list of receivables balances.	✓	
A payment from a customer of £230 had accidentally been posted as £320 to their individual account in the receivables ledger.	✓	

7 **PURCHASES LEDGER CONTROL ACCOUNT RECONCILIATION**

	Add/Subtract	£
Total from list of balances		132,589
Adjustment for (a)	Add	445
Adjustment for (b)	Subtract	4,340
Adjustment for (c)	Subtract	1,200
Adjustment for (d)	Subtract	132
Adjustment for (e)	Add	2,100
Adjustment for (f)	Add	120
Revised total to agree with PLCA		129,582

8 **ERRORS**

(a) **Journal**

	Dr £	Cr £
Motor expenses	4,500	
Motor vehicles at cost		4,500

(b) **Journal**

	Dr £	Cr £
Office sundries	16	
Suspense		16

(c)   Journal

	Dr £	Cr £
Closing inventory – statement of financial position	42,000	
Closing inventory – statement of profit or loss		42,000

Working

Inventory is valued at the lower of cost and net realisable value. The selling price is given as £50,400. To get to the selling price, 20% of the value of the cost is added to the cost. The cost of £42,000 has been calculated by dividing the selling price by 120 and then multiplying by 100. (50,400/120) × 100 = 42,000.

The value of closing inventory, in accordance with IAS 2 is £42,000.

(d)   Journal

	Dr £	Cr £
Receivables	1,720	
Discounts allowed		1,720
Discounts allowed	1,270	
Receivables		1,270

9   CHANGEOVER

Which TWO of the following controls can mitigate the risk of system failure during direct changeover?

Testing	✓
Training	
System documentation	
Data backup	✓
Check digits	

Note: Testing reduces the probability of failure, and data backup reduces the impact.

10 INFORMATION SYSTEM CONTROLS

	Security	Integrity
Locked doors	✓	
Passwords	✓	
Batch totals		✓
Reconciliation		✓
CCTV	✓	
Check digits		✓
Authorisation of data entry		✓
Fire alarms	✓	

11 PURCHASE CYCLE CONTROLS 1

Which TWO of the following controls in a purchase cycle could be implemented to reduce the risk of payment of goods not received?

Sequentially pre-numbered purchase requisitions and sequence check.	
Matching of goods received note with purchase invoice.	✓
Goods are inspected for condition and quantity and agreed to purchase order before acceptance.	✓
Daily update of inventory system.	

12 PURCHASE CYCLE CONTROLS 2

Which TWO of the following controls in the purchase cycle could be implemented to reduce the risk of procurement of unnecessary goods and services?

Centralised purchasing department.	✓
Sequentially pre-numbered purchase requisitions and sequence check.	
Orders can only be placed with suppliers from the approved suppliers list.	
All purchase requisitions are signed as authorised by an appropriate manager.	✓

13 EXPENSE CLAIM CONTROLS

Which ONE of the following essential internal control measures is evidently missing?

AEM Ltd lacks a control environment as the board are not setting an ethical tone at the top.	✓
AEM Ltd lacks an Internal Audit department.	
AEM Ltd lacks an experienced finance manager.	
AEM Ltd lacks an external auditor.	

14 PASSWORDS 1

Which of the following would be the most secure?

24june1963	
LaraJo	
mypassword	
Qwerty123!#	✓

15 PASSWORDS 2

Which TWO of the following would reduce the effectiveness of passwords?

Requirement that passwords are changed every two weeks	
Users are allowed to choose their own passwords	✓
Automatic lock-out after 3 failed attempts to access system	
Making the sharing of passwords a disciplinary offence	
Displaying the password on the screen when entered	✓

16 INTERNAL CONTROLS 1

Match each of the following activities to the component that it illustrates.

	Control environment	Information system	Control activities
The process of preparing the financial statements		✓	
Locking the inventory storeroom			✓

17 INTERNAL CONTROLS 2

Match each of the following activities to the type of control that it illustrates.

	Authorisation	Information processing	Physical control
The financial controller will count petty cash on a weekly basis			✓
There will be two keys to the locked safe: one held by the FD and the other by the CEO.			✓

18 INTERNAL CONTROLS 3

Match each of the following activities to the type of computer control that it illustrates.

	General	Application
Storing extra copies of programs and data files off-site	✓	
New programmes to check data fields on input transactions		✓
Manual checks to ensure that input data were authorised		✓
Password protection limiting access to data	✓	
Range checks on payroll processing		✓
Manual checks to ensure that timesheets are authorised before details are processed		✓

19 INTERNAL CONTROLS 4

Indicate whether the following limitations are true or false.

	True	False
The cost of implementing controls may be more expensive than the benefits gained due to reduced risk	✓	
The effectiveness of many controls rely on the integrity of those applying them	✓	
Internal controls are only applied to material items		✓
Standard controls may not be designed to deal with unusual transactions	✓	

20 FRAUD 1

Which TWO of the following would best reduce the risk of this fraud occurring?

Segregation of duties between cash payments and recording at head office	
Post opening by two people	
Daily reconciliation of recorded till sales and cash taken in the showroom	✓
Regular banking of cash and cheques received in the showroom	✓

21 FRAUD 2

Which ONE of the following control activities would best prevent this occurring?

Payroll standing data periodically printed out and checked on a line-by-line basis to independently held employee details	
Use of hierarchical passwords over standing data files	✓
Pre-authorisation of all amendments to payroll standing data by an independent official	
Supervision of the wages pay out by an independent official	

Note: In order to prevent this from happening, the key is that fictitious employees never make it onto the payroll.

- Printing out and checking standing data will detect any fictitious employees added but will not prevent them from being added.

- Use of hierarchical passwords over standing data files ensures that an unscrupulous employee cannot access the part of the system where new employees would be added and hence will prevent the fraud. This is therefore the correct answer.

- Pre-authorisation of all amendments will not prevent the addition as an unscrupulous employee will not ask for authorisation but will simply add the fictitious details if the system allows them to do this.

- Supervision of the wages pay out by an independent official might detect dummy employees but would be unlikely to prevent the fraud.

TASK 1.2

Assessment objective 2	Evaluate budgetary reporting; its effectiveness in controlling and improving organisational performance.

22 TRAINING COSTS

(a) **BRIEFLY discuss THREE weaknesses in the above use of performance reports to improve the focus of training within AEM Ltd.**

Weakness 1
Flexing
The budget is a fixed one; meaning it has not been flexed for the 25% increase in activity.
A flexible budget is one where the turnover and variable costs are changed in line with the change in activity. In this case they would be increased by 25%. Fixed costs remain unchanged from the original budget.
The advantage of fixed budgeting is that it takes less time and is, therefore, less costly to produce; the disadvantage is that variances are less meaningful and, therefore, control is effectively reduced. The advantage and disadvantage of flexible budgeting are the opposite of this.
The flexed budget cost would be
$$13,000 + 1,000 \times (25/20) = £14,250$$
This gives an overall favourable variance of £150 rather than an adverse one of £100. The manager should thus be praised rather than reprimanded.

Weakness 2
Participation in target setting and budgeting
Petr Higgs was not involved in setting the original budget and did not even know about it. This lack of participation could easily result in him viewing the target as unfair and unrealistic, resulting in demotivation. It is also very difficult to be motivated to hit a target you are unaware of!
Greater participation will help resolve these issues and also may result in more realistic budgets in the first place. The main disadvantage of participation is the possibility of budget "padding", where Petr may have tried to set an easy target for himself.

Weakness 3
Emphasis on financial factors
The sole emphasis on financial factors only may result in Petr being more concerned about cost control than delivering high quality training.
The directors were concerned that training lacked focus rather than it being too expensive. There is nothing in the email to see if focus has improved.

Weakness 4
Lauren Bristow's tone
Lauren Bristow's tone is far too aggressive, particularly given the above factors, and is likely to result in resentment and demotivation.
This is particularly the case as it is the first month of the new system, so there is a significant possibility that budgeted figures are not representative in the first place. The variance could thus be due to planning errors rather than Petr's operational performance.

(b) Outline THREE performance indicators that could be used to assess the quality of the training provided.

Performance Indicator 1
Trainee feedback
Trainees could be asked to score different elements of the training process on a score of 1 to 5 say. This would indicate whether or not they felt the training was useful to them and would indicate areas for improvement.

Performance Indicator 2
Manager feedback
Presumably managers had objectives when sending staff on training courses/events – for example, to give better advice to customers on customer service. Managers could be asked to assess whether they felt that their staff had benefited from the training – for example, were they more able to undertake required tasks in their roles? Again, a score of 1 to 5 would allow easier monitoring of feedback.

Performance Indicator 3
Objective scoring using tests
For some training – for example, awareness of GDPR legislation – it may be possible to set a quiz or test before and after training to see if trainee's knowledge and awareness had improved.

(Total 15 marks)

23 BUDGETING

Evaluate the budget for 20X3 by discussing the following assumed (or implied) growth rates. In your answer discuss whether or not you feel the figures are realistic and why.

(15 marks)

Figure	Whether or not realistic
Sales volume growth of 35.2%	*Arguments for*
	Acquisition of WV Ltd increased the number of showrooms by 4, an increase of 27%. In addition, AEM must be planning to open a further 2 showrooms to take the total up to 21.
	The average number of cars sold per showroom is expected to fall from 147 (2200/15) in X2 to 142 (2975/21), so the high growth cannot be interpreted as the result of unrealistic sales targets for showroom mangers.
	On top of this, growth in industry demand is expected to be 20%
	Finally, there should be increasing brand awareness due to the award.
	Arguments against
	An economic downturn is predicted.
	WV Ltd is not known for selling electric vehicles so its showrooms will not benefit from the growth in these.
	The additional 2 new showrooms will not have a full impact on sales volumes due to (1) being opened part way through the year and (2) needing time to build a local presence.
Sales revenue growth of 22.6%	Compared to volume growth of 35.2%, revenue growth of 22.6% seems even more reasonable. The difference is mainly due to the average price per car decreasing by 7.6%.
	This could be due to a fall in the average price resulting from required price cuts as part of price-matching guarantees, discounts to attract new customers or price cuts as a response to increased competition in an economic downturn.
	Finally, lower average prices could be due to a change is sales mix, especially towards used cars rather than new. This is highly likely due to WV Ltd only selling used cars at present.
Cost of sales growth of 17.1%	Cost of sales growth of only 17.1% seems low compared to sales volume growth of 35.2%.
	One way of explaining this difference between them would only be feasible if a significant proportion of cost of sales were fixed costs rather than variable. This seems unlikely as the main part of cost of sales will be the purchase cost of cars and parts.
	A more likely explanation is the shift towards selling relatively more used cars than new as the former will be significantly cheaper to buy.

| Growth in operating expenses of 19.0% | Operating costs are likely to be mainly fixed in nature, so the increase will be mainly due to the acquisition of WV Ltd as this will men two head-offices, two finance teams, and so on, as well as the increase in showrooms. |
| | We are not told whether WV's head office and warehouse will be closed down as part of the integration of the two businesses. |

Conclusion – whether or not the budget is realistic

| Overall the budget looks reasonable in terms of sales growth and cost behaviour, especially if plans to open new showrooms are fully implemented in time to impact the budget to the degree shown. |

24 AEM LTD'S BUDGETING PROCESS

Strengths

- Inflation should be allowed for as this leads to more accurate budgets

- Wages and product costs seem to be accounted for correctly

- Marketing seems to be based on only those areas that the directors wish to specifically promote, reducing the possibility of cost overspends or unfocussed marketing expenditure

- Some attempt is made to account for the effectiveness of the marketing spend using regression analysis

Weaknesses

- Whilst choice over RPI and CPI is good for motivation it can lead to inconsistency and confusion for managers that are unaware of the difference and appropriateness of these.

- No inflationary guidance is given for costs other than wages and product costs implying that these other costs are "minor". This therefore excludes, for example, IT and website costs, which are significant.

- Past inflation is not necessarily equal to future inflation – for example, after the Covid pandemic, UK inflation jumped considerably compared to past measures.

- Showroom managers are not consulted on any specific marketing need. This can be demotivating and might not address concerns over poor performance – for example, a rival may be offering higher discounts for electric cars but senior management have not incorporated this.

- It is unclear how total budgets are allocated – for example, Jenni Black may feel that AEM Ltd needs to spend more promoting its online presence

- Past marketing to sales trends may not continue given the ever-changing markets

- Sales volumes change for other reasons (not just marketing)

Opportunities

- A central decision should be made regarding the inflation measure to be used

- More complete inflationary guidance could be given to include all costs lines

- Greater account could be given to current market conditions when predicting sales (rather than relying purely on past regression)

Threats

- If inflation is under-estimated, then this could lead to an under budgeted costs and adverse variances. The opposite is true for over-estimated inflation

- Omission of inflationary guidance for (in particular) IT costs could lead to a significant budget error, loss of confidence in the process and under funding

- Sales levels may disappoint if no showroom-specific considerations are made

- Assuming that the past will continue into the future is misguided and new opportunities may be missed or complacency could set in

- Budget sales levels could be incorrect leading to poor assumptions about profitability

TASK 1.3

Assessment objective 3	Evaluate an organisation's accounting control systems and procedures.

25 WV LTD'S PURCHASING SYSTEM

Required:

Identify and explain FOUR deficiencies in the system, explain the possible implication of each deficiency and provide a recommendation to address each deficiency. **(15 marks)**

Deficiency	Implication	Recommendation
When raising purchase orders, the clerks choose whichever supplier can dispatch the goods the fastest.	This could result in Weldon Vehicles Ltd ordering goods at a much higher price or a lower quality than they would like, as the only factor considered was speed of delivery. It is important that goods are dispatched promptly, but this is just one of many criteria that should be used in deciding which supplier to use.	An approved supplier list should be compiled; this should take into account the price of goods, their quality and also the speed of delivery. Once the list has been produced, all orders should only be placed with suppliers on the approved list.

Deficiency	Implication	Recommendation
Purchase orders are not sequentially numbered.	Failing to sequentially number the orders means that Weldon Vehicles Ltd's ordering team is unable to monitor if all orders are being fulfilled in a timely manner; this could result in stock outs. If the orders are numbered, then a sequence check can be performed for any unfulfilled orders.	All purchase orders should be sequentially numbered and on a regular basis a sequence check of unfulfilled orders should be performed.
Purchase orders below £100 are not authorised and are processed solely by an order clerk.	This can result in goods being purchased which are not required by Weldon Vehicles Ltd. In addition, there is an increased fraud risk as an order clerk could place orders for personal goods up to the value of £100, which is significant.	All purchase orders should be authorised by a responsible official. Authorised signatories should be established with varying levels of purchase order authorisation.
Purchase invoices are input daily by the purchase ledger clerk and due to his experience, he does not utilise any application controls.	Without application controls there is a risk that invoices could be input into the system with inaccuracies or they may be missed out entirely. This could result in suppliers being paid incorrectly or not all, leading to a loss of supplier goodwill.	The purchase ledger clerk should input the invoices in batches and apply application controls, such as control totals, to ensure completeness and accuracy over the input of purchase invoices.
The purchase day book automatically updates with the purchase ledger but this ledger is manually posted to the general ledger.	Manually posting the amounts to the general ledger increases the risk of errors occurring. This could result in the payables balance in the financial statements being under or overstated.	The process should be updated so that on a regular basis the purchase ledger automatically updates the general ledger. A responsible official should then confirm through purchase ledger control account reconciliations that the update has occurred correctly.

Deficiency	Implication	Recommendation
Weldon Vehicles Ltd's saving (deposit) bank accounts are only reconciled every two months.	If these accounts are only reconciled periodically, there is the risk that errors will not be spotted promptly. Also, this increases the risk of employees committing fraud. If they are aware that these accounts are not regularly reviewed, then they could use these cash sums fraudulently.	All bank accounts should be reconciled on a regular basis, and at least monthly, to identify any unusual or missing items. The reconciliations should be reviewed by a responsible official and they should evidence their review.
Weldon Vehicles Ltd has a policy of delaying payments to their suppliers for as long as possible.	Whilst this maximises Weldon Vehicles Ltd's bank balance, there is the risk that Weldon Vehicles Ltd is missing out on early settlement discounts. Also, this can lead to a loss of supplier goodwill as well as the risk that suppliers may refuse to supply goods to Weldon Vehicles Ltd or send lower quality consumables, for example.	Weldon Vehicles Ltd should undertake cash flow forecasting/ budgeting to maximise bank balances. The policy of delaying payment should be reviewed, and suppliers should be paid in a systematic way, such that supplier goodwill is not lost.

26 WV LTD'S CASH RECEIPTS AND PAYMENTS PROCESSES

Required:

Identify and explain FIVE DEFICIENCIES in Weldon Vehicles Ltd's cash receipts and payments system and provide a recommendation to address each of these deficiencies.

(15 marks)

Control deficiency	Recommendation
To speed up the cash payment by customers, the tills have the same log on code and these codes are changed fortnightly. In the event of cash discrepancies arising in the tills, it would be difficult to ascertain which employees may be responsible as there is no way of tracking who used which till. This could lead to cash being easily misappropriated.	Each employee should be provided with a unique log on code and this is required to be entered when using the tills. In order to facilitate the investigation of till differences, employees should be allocated to a specific till point for their shift. Any discrepancies which arise should initially be double checked to ensure they are not arithmetical errors. If still present, the relevant employees who had access to the till can be identified and further investigations can be undertaken.

Control deficiency	Recommendation
The reconciliations of the tills to the daily sales readings are performed in total for all three tills rather than for each till. This means that when exceptions arise, it will be difficult to identify which till caused the difference. This increases the risk of staff undertaking fraudulent transactions.	The reconciliations should be undertaken on an individual till by till basis rather than in aggregate and any discrepancies noted should be investigated immediately. Furthermore, employees may require further till training.
The cashing up of tills along with the recording of any cash discrepancies is undertaken by just one individual, the showroom manager. There is a fraud risk as the manager could remove some of the cash and then simply record that there was an exception on the daily sales list. In addition, as there is no segregation of duties, the manager could, fraudulently or by error, record the total sales as per each till incorrectly leading to incorrect identification of discrepancies.	The cashing up process should be undertaken by two individuals together. One should count the cash and the other record it. Any exceptions to the till reading should be double checked to confirm that they are not simply arithmetical errors. If still present, the relevant employees who had access to the till can be identified and further investigations can be undertaken.
Daily sales sheets are scanned and emailed to head office on a weekly basis. There is a possibility that some sales sheets could be misplaced by the showroom manager. This will result in incomplete sales and cash receipts data being recorded into the accounting system.	Daily sales sheets should be sequentially numbered and remitted to head office on a daily basis. Someone in the accounts department could then perform a sequence check should be undertaken on a regular basis to identify any missing sheets and any gaps should be investigated further. Once received, Maisie should post the sales and cash data on a daily basis. Once processed, they should then be signed as posted by Maisie and filed away securely.
Cash is stored in a safe and the manager stores the safe key in a drawer of their desk when not in use. Although cash is banked on a daily basis, there could still be a significant sum of cash onsite each day, especially if cars have been bought for cash. There is a risk of significant cash losses due to theft if access to the safe key is not carefully controlled.	The current key lock safe should be replaced with a safe with a digital code. Only authorised personnel should have the code which should be updated on a regular basis.

Control deficiency	Recommendation
The General Accounts Clerk, Maisie Fox, is responsible for several elements of the cash receipts system. She receives the daily sales sheets, agrees that cash has cleared into the bank statements, updates the cash book and undertakes the bank reconciliations. There is a lack of segregation of duties and errors will not be identified on a timely basis.	These key roles should be split between different members of the finance team, with ideally the bank reconciliations being undertaken by another member of the team.
Maisie is not checking that payments made by credit card have resulted in cash being received by Weldon Vehicles Ltd. The credit card statements are not reviewed or reconciled, they are just filed away. There is a risk that receipts of cash by credit card may have been omitted and this would not be identified on a timely basis as the bank is only reconciled every two months. This may result in difficulties in resolving any discrepancies with the credit card company.	Maisie should reconcile the credit card vouchers to the monthly statement received from the card company. The daily amounts per the statement should be agreed to the bank statement to ensure that all funds have been received. This reconciliation should be reviewed by a responsible official, such as a financial controller, who should evidence by signature that the review has been undertaken.
The bank reconciliations are only carried out every two months. If it is not reconciled regularly enough, then this reduces its effectiveness as fraud and errors may not be identified on a timely basis.	The bank reconciliations should be performed on a monthly basis rather than every two months. The financial controller should continue to review each reconciliation and evidence his review by way of signature on the bank reconciliation.
The finance director only views the total amount of payments to be made rather than the amounts to be paid to each supplier. Without looking at the detail of the payments list, as well as supporting documentation, there is a risk that suppliers could be being paid an incorrect amount, or that sums are being paid to fictitious suppliers. This will cause loss for the company.	The finance director should review the whole payments list prior to authorising. As part of this, he should agree the amounts to be paid to supporting documentation, as well as reviewing the supplier names to identify any duplicates or any unfamiliar names. He should evidence his review by signing the bank transfer list.

Note: only FIVE required.

27   AEM LTD'S INVENTORY COUNTING PROCESSES

Weakness	Effect of Weakness
The external auditor should attend as an observer only and not get involved in the count itself. To do so confuses the roles of the people involved.	Errors in process might not have been detected as the internal auditor was busy "doing" rather than "observing". It is also possible that the auditor who is not an employee is not competent to recognize damaged or slow moving inventory and so these items could go unrecorded.
The instructions are capable of misinterpretation. Staff seem to have been instructed to record all items that are shown on the sheets as being in a certain location. They might not record items that are therefore in the wrong location, or only look in designated locations rather than all possible places where inventory may be held.	This could lead to serious understatement of the inventory values and hence an understatement of profit.
The designation of duties is a little unclear. The two unallocated zones appear to fall between two counting teams and so the count is then dependent on the organisation of the spare resource on the count day.	An area could either be missed or be counted by both teams. This could lead to over or under statement of the inventory and hence profit.
The delivery that took place on the day of the count might not have been accounted for properly. It is not clear from the question what happened to the actual counting of the delivery. The items should have been included, even though they were in the car park at the time. Equally, details of the delivery should have been recorded so that correct cut off with regards to purchases could subsequently be checked.	The items could have been incorrectly excluded and so inventory understated. Without delivery details being recorded a cut off error could have occurred. Consistency between the recording of inventory and the recording of purchases is important and without this the incorrect profit will be calculated.
Box labelling was relied on for the contents of boxes. This is an unreliable method. Damaged items within the boxes would not be identified.	Inventory could be misstated as the content of the boxes might not reflect the labelling. If damaged items are not identified then the inventory will be overstated.
Old items (slow-moving) were not identified or recorded during the count.	The accounting policy cannot be checked against the actual figures and so AEM Ltd might not detect and error in that policy.

Note: only FIVE required.

TASK 1.4

Assessment objective 4	Analyse an organisation's decision making and control using management accounting tools.

28 STOCKING DECISIONS

(a) BRIEFLY discuss the validity of each of the three directors' views on how the final decision should be made as to pack options to prioritise. **(9 marks)**

Chief Executive
The Chief Executive is basing decisions on the reported profits of each product. The reported operating profits include an arbitrary allocation of fixed costs that undermines their credibility.
While the Chief Executive is correct that fixed costs must be covered somewhere, they are irrelevant to the decision as they are by definition unavoidable regardless of the decision.
Decisions should be made on the basis of future incremental cash flows.

Sales Director
The Sales Director is basing decisions on the contribution of each product. This has the advantage of considering only the future relevant cash flows and ignoring the allocated fixed overheads.
Looking at total contribution would only be appropriate if there was enough space to stock sufficient packs to meet full demand, which is not the case here.
Unit contribution would be appropriate if all packs involved the same amount of space, but, again, this is not the case here.

Finance Director
The Finance Director has the best overall approach as she is considering contribution, thus looking at relevant cash flows and ignoring allocated overheads.
In addition, and unlike the Sales Director, she is then incorporating how much space is needed to store each filter. The ranking based on contribution per unit of scarce resource (i.e. square metres of storage) should ensure that the use of the space is maximised to generate the most contribution possible.

(b) BRIEFLY explain THREE other factors should be taken into consideration before making a final decision. **(6 marks)**

Factor 1
How much space is available
The directors' comments suggest that the decision is focussed on selecting just one filter to stock. However, it may be that there is sufficient space to offer a number of options, even if there is not enough for all of them.
For example, stocking 40 Ds would need 40 × 0.110 = 4.4 sq.m. This is sufficient for all of the Cs (requires 20 × 0.102 = 2.4) and a significant number of Bs, say.
Furthermore, it may be possible to increase the amount of available storage by using spare capacity at other showrooms and using couriers to move filters as and when required.

Factor 2
Requirements planning and solutions
Most customers will book cars in for services many weeks before required. This could allow WV to operate a just in time approach to ordering filters in time for when they are needed, rather than holding large inventories.
For emergency work at short notice, WV could pay a premium to have the required parts delivered from suppliers at short notice, negating the need for inventory.

29   CLOSURE OF SHOWROOM

(a)   **Assess the decision using relevant cash flows**   **(9 marks)**

Contribution lost from the combined firms - AEM

- Total contribution for 20X3 = 2,400 × 60/160 = 900

- Contribution lost if closed = 20% × 900 = (180)

Contribution lost from the combined firms - WV

- Total contribution for 20X3 = 2,250 × 50/150 = 750

- Contribution lost if closed = 30% × 750 = (225)

Closure costs are fully incremental

- AEM: (70)

- WV: (60)

Labour costs saved due to redundancies

- AEM: Saving = 75 × 80% = 60 per annum

- WV: Saving = 65 × 80% = 52 per annum

Overhead costs saved (excluding head office costs incurred anyway)

- AEM: Saving = 125 - 10 = 115 per annum

- WV: Saving = 122 - 8 = 114 per annum

Overall impact of closure

- AEM: Net cash flow = (180) + (70) + 60 + 115 = (75)

- WV: Net cash flow = (225) + (60) + 52 + 114 = (119)

Comments

- Both net cash flows are negative suggesting that plans to close either showroom should be rejected.

- If we have to close a showroom, then closing AEM showroom #12 makes more sense financially, mainly due to the lower level of lost contribution that would result.

(b) Briefly explain three other factors that need to be considered. **(6 marks)**

Factor 1 - Impact on staff morale for WV
• Integrating the two businesses and change management will always be stressful for staff involved, especially those of the company taken over (here, WV).
• Closing the WV showroom may result in WV staff feeling undervalued and wondering what other cuts they will suffer.
Factor 2 – Impact on customers and marketing costs
• The analysis assumes that most of the sales for one showroom will be picked up by the other, limiting lost contribution.
• However, without extensive marketing to potential customers, they are unlikely to have any loyalty to the other business. There must be reasons why one would go to WV rather than AEM or vice versa.
Factor 3 – Redundancy costs
• As far as staff costs are concerned, the analysis only considers wages saved and ignores redundancy costs
• While AEM is a young business and staff would have few years' service, WV may have some staff who have been there much longer and hence entitled to larger pay-outs.

30 AEM LTD PLANNING

(a) Data table:

Quarter Number (X)	Quarter ended	Cars sold (Y)	Revenue £000	Variable Cost £000	Contribution £000
1	30/9/X1	35	875	350	525
2	31/12/X1	29	725	290	435
3	31/3/X2	27	675	270	450
4	30/6/X2	26	650	260	390
5	30/9/X2	24	600	240	360
6	31/12/X2	24	600	240	360
7	31/3/X3	21	525	210	315
8	30/6/X3	19	475	190	285
9	30/9/X3	17	425	170	255
10	31/12/X3	15	375	150	225

Working: cost per car = 25,000 × 0.40 = £10,000

*[Note: the first 6 quarters are **actual** results so would not be expected to fit the regression line exactly.]*

(b) **Discussion of findings:**

The value 'b'

The value b is the slope of the regression line, indicating by how much the value y declines (in this case) and the x value increases by 1 (1 quarter in this case). Hence it shows that sales volume is expected to decline by 2 cars per quarter for the HX6 as time ticks by. This is based on the average of past declines and there is no guarantee that past trend reflects the future. The decline could be greater or lower than the 2 cars given.

Data findings

The data shows that this product's revenue will fall to £375,000 by the end of the planning horizon (Quarter ended 31/12/X3). Over the same period the contribution gained also gradually falls and reaches only £225,000 by that same point.

The important point is that AEM Ltd will continue to make a positive contribution up to that quarter and so should be willing to continue to supply the product.

The data also states that this product's share of fixed costs are £250,000 and this might imply to some that cessation of supply is justified as the model will be loss making. However, it must be borne in mind that these fixed costs will not be avoidable on cessation and as such are not relevant to a cessation decision.

If they were directly attributable, then they would be relevant.

Furthermore, the data only relates to sales of that model and does not include sales of other cars that might increase were this model discontinued.

(c) **Non-financial considerations (2 needed)**

Businesses should not make all decisions purely based on the financial figures and this case is no different. The following considerations are worthy of note:

Impact on range offered – it would be important to replace the model with a similarly priced and spec'd model to ensure a complete range is offered. Presumably Ford will have a replacement within their range of electric cars.

Impact on staff – presumably some sales staff have become experts in the features of this particular model and will need additional training if replacements are adopted.

Nature of decision – the decision is not set in stone – for example, given the new cars are bought rather than made, it would be relatively easy to sell this model again if a customer enquires about it.

TASK 1.5

AO5	Analyse an organisation's decision making and control using ratio analysis.

31 OVERTRADING

(a) Complete the scorecard by calculating the missing ratios. **(10 marks)**

AEM Ltd (excluding WV Ltd) Scorecard	X3	X2
Profitability and gearing		
Gross profit %	27.5%	28.5%
Operating profit %	6.6%	5.9%
Return on capital employed	38.8%	42.2%
Gearing (debt/equity)	1.62×	1.31×
Liquidity ratios		
Current ratio	3.28:1	2.05:1
Acid test/Quick ratio	1.26:1	0.57:1
Working capital days		
Inventory holding period	64 days	62 days
Trade receivables collection period	12 days	9 days
Trade payables payment period	32 days	38 days
Working capital operating cycle	44 days	33 days

(b) Select the ONE correct observation about each aspect of business performance below. **(10 marks)**

Profitability

20X3 will be a year of steady, if unspectacular, progress. Although margins have dipped, the return on capital employed has been kept constant.	
The changes in gross margin could be due to cost control problems concerning distribution.	
Increased competition and the resulting pressure on prices could explain the change in each of the three profitability ratios.	✓

Gearing

The increased gearing ratio proves that the company has no problems raising additional debt finance.	
It is likely that the interest cover ratio has increased.	
The increased gearing ratio shows that the shareholders' position has become more risky.	✓

Liquidity

Both ratios have increased, which indicates that the company is less solvent.	
A higher quick ratio is a clear indicator of overtrading.	
The change in both the current and quick ratios could be partly explained by the increase in the receivables period.	✓

Working capital

The working capital cycle has worsened. This increases the possibility of AEM overtrading.	✓
There is a welcome improvement in the working capital cycle, mainly due to the change in the payment period for payables.	
The working capital cycle is worse than a year ago, solely because of the change in inventory days.	

Overall performance

Despite overall growth, AEM is expected to have a difficult year in 20X3 and needs to investigate why key ratios will be deteriorating.	✓
20X3 looks to be a disaster for AEM.	
There is no evidence of possible control problems.	

32 ANALYSIS OF WV LTD

(a) **Complete the scorecard.**   (10 marks)

20X9	AEM	WV
Profitability		
Gross profit %	28.5%	**49.3%**
Operating profit %	5.9%	9.5%
Return on capital employed	42.2%	**27.9%**
Liquidity ratios		
Current ratio	2.1:1	**2.0:1**
Acid test/Quick ratio	0.6:1	0.6:1
Working capital days		
Inventory holding period	62 days	60 days
Trade receivables collection period	9 days	12 days
Trade payables payment period	38 days	**30 days**
Working capital cycle	33 days	**42 days**

(b) Assess the following statements. (10 marks)

Statement	True	False	Comment
The difference in gross margins could be explained by WV Ltd offering a 50% discount on servicing for two years on all cars sold.		✓	A 50% discount on servicing will give WV a lower GPM, not a higher one.
If AEM Ltd has delayed paying suppliers at the year end, then this would contribute to the difference in current ratios.		✓	AEM would have both higher cash and payables, making its current ratio nearer to 1.
The difference in the ROCE figures could be explained by the fact that WV Ltd is much older than AEM Ltd.	✓		Being older, WV would have more retained profits and so higher equity
A warehouse employee in AEM Ltd was found to have stolen spare parts and given them to friends. This would contribute to the difference in the ROCE figures.		✓	Theft would give AEM a lower GPM and, viewed in isolation, a lower ROCE
Inadequate controls over expense claims for managers within TW Ltd could contribute to the difference in the operating margins figures.		✓	This would give WV a lower operating margin, not a higher one.

33   CASH AND PROFIT

Why is profit important in business? (5 marks)

Profits are the generally accepted measure of the successful trading of a business.

Profit is the most commonly used measure of performance with analysts looking at figures for profit, profit margins and return on capital employed. As such the determination of profit is heavily regulated.

This regulation (in the form of standard accounting practices) ensures that all companies measure profit is broadly the same way and in this way, it is trusted by investors (such as the venture capitalists) and management to reflect performance.

The press often focusses on profitability when commenting on a business's performance and this tends to increase the profile of the profit measure on all concerned.

Why must cash also be considered in business? (5 marks)

Cash in this context is the cash balance of the business at any one time and also the amount of cash the business has generated or spent over the accounting period.

Cash is seen as vital in business for a number of reasons:

Cash is used for investment. If a business wants to buy assets in order to grow, then it needs cash to do that.

It can borrow that money, that is true, but in this case it will need cash to make the repayments on any loan it takes out.

Cash is also used to make normal commercial payments. Wages, suppliers, and rent, all must be paid for with cash and so without cash these payments cannot be made and trade would stop.

The government also have a stake in businesses and although the regulation insists that profits are measured the government requires that corporate tax is paid. Although the amount of tax is in part determined by the profits made the company needs cash to actually make the payment.

Cash might also be needed for emergencies, to cover for example unexpected payments. Businesses often hold reserves of cash for this purpose.

Does the cash equal the profit? (5 marks)

In some ways, what Barbara says is true. If the company buys consumables from a supplier, then that will have to be paid for. However, one important difference here is the timing of the purchase compared to the payment. There is often a lag between the purchase and the subsequent payment. Consequently, although the two figures are the same they will be recorded at different points of time.

Also, there are other cash transactions that are not reflected in the profits of the business immediately. For example, when a business buys new shelving for the warehouse, the cash outflow would be immediate and in total. The expense in the profit and loss account would slowly catch up over a number of years as depreciation is charged over the assets useful economic life but there would be a significant delay in the case of long existing assets.

The final major difference created between cash and profits is dividend. Dividend is a cash outflow but does not go through the profit and loss account at all.

For all the above reasons the amount a business has in cash is not equal to the profitability of the same business. In extreme cases, companies can be guilty of 'over-trading' – trying to grow too quickly and run out of cash despite being profitable.

Discuss whether delaying the rent payments will be effective in increasing profits and the ethical stance the accounting department should take to the request. (5 marks)

The accounts of a business are produced using generally accepted accounting principles. One of these is matching. The principle is that over an accounting period expense are related to that period regardless of the cash transactions.

What this means is that if a rent payment is delayed (as is being suggested in this case) then it would still be necessary to reflect the full rent cost in the profit and loss account and an accrual entry would be made to record it.

Consequently, delaying the rent payment would not be effective in increasing profits.

Ethically the accounts staff will be bound by an ethical code and would therefore be expected to behave professionally and with due care. Where it is being suggested that an accounting error (i.e. not posting the rent to boost profit) be deliberately made in order to manipulate the accounts then the accountants would have to resist and in some way refuse to make the adjustment.

TASK 1.6

Assessment objective 6	Analyse the internal controls of an organisation and make recommendations.

34 WELDON VEHICLES LTD'S PAYROLL SYSTEMS

Identify and explain FIVE DEFICIENCIES in Weldon Vehicles Ltd's payroll system, and provide a recommendation to address each of these deficiencies. **(15 marks)**

Deficiency	Recommendation
Employees are not given a contract of employment. Staff could be under or over paid, or not work their contracted hours. This could result in disputes over terms of employment, leading to compensation being paid, or costs involved in employment tribunals.	All staff should be given a contract of employment which they are required to sign before commencing work. Existing staff should also be given a new contract as soon as possible.
The time recording machine is not in view and the clocking in/out process is not supervised. This could result in staff clocking in or out for their colleagues and the company paying for hours that have not been worked. This will increase payroll costs and cash outflows of the company.	The time recording machine should be relocated to where it is in view by other staff and the warehouse manager. The clocking in and out process should be supervised by the warehouse manager. Alternatively, a CCTV camera could be installed to record the clocking in and out process.
Spare clock cards are kept in the rack with the cards being used by staff. Staff could use the spare cards to create a duplicate wage claim. This will increase payroll costs and cash outflows of the company.	Spare clock cards should be kept locked away from the time recording machine. Staff should request a new one if theirs becomes damaged. The Payroll Manager should regularly reconcile the number of active clock cards to the number of current staff, or perform a one to one check of named employees on cards, to staff records.
Employees take time to have a meal or drink once they have clocked in. Employees may take excessive meal breaks resulting in the company paying for time not worked. This will increase costs and cash outflows.	If the provision of meals is to continue, staff should be requested not to clock on until after they have finished their meal. The hours worked can be increased by a specified meal break time allowance e.g. 20 minutes.

Deficiency	Recommendation
The weekly clock cards are sent for processing with no checks or authorisation being undertaken. If staff have been fraudulently recording hours worked, this will not be picked up before the payments are made, unless by the Payroll Manager. This will increase costs and cash outflows for the company.	Before being sent off, the warehouse manager should review the clock cards for accuracy and sign to approve the hours worked. Before authorising payment, the Payroll Manager should review the hours worked for reasonableness and investigate any significant discrepancies.
No checks are made on data submitted to the shared google doc by home workers. This means staff could fraudulently record more hours than they actually worked, resulting in excessive overtime claims.	Staff should be asked to contact their line managers for approval before any overtime is worked. Such authorisation should be copied to the payroll manager in advance. The company could install software that allows them to monitor company laptop activity to see if people are working when they say they are

Note: only FIVE required

35 DALE HOME CHARGING LTD'S SALES AND DESPATCH SYSTEM

Identify and explain FIVE deficiencies in Dale Ltd's sales and despatch system and provide a recommendation to address each of these deficiencies. **(15 marks)**

Deficiency	Recommendation
Inventory availability for telephone orders is not checked at the time the order is placed. The order clerks manually check the availability later and only then inform customers if there is insufficient inventory available. There is the risk that where goods are not available, order clerks could forget to contact the customers, leading to unfulfilled orders. This could lead to customer dissatisfaction, and would impact the firm's reputation.	When telephone orders are placed, the order clerk should check the inventory system whilst the customer is on the phone; they can then give an accurate assessment of the availability of goods and there is no risk of forgetting to inform customers.

Deficiency	Recommendation
Telephone orders are not recorded immediately on the three-part pre-printed order forms; these are completed after the telephone call. There is a risk that incorrect or insufficient details may be recorded by the clerk and this could result in incorrect orders being despatched or orders failing to be despatched at all, resulting in a loss of customer goodwill.	All telephone orders should be recorded immediately on the three-part pre-printed order forms. The clerk should also double check all the details taken with the customer over the telephone to ensure the accuracy of the order recorded.
Telephone orders are not sequentially numbered. Therefore if orders are misplaced whilst in transit to the despatch department, these orders will not be fulfilled, resulting in dissatisfied customers.	The three part pre-printed orders forms should be sequentially numbered and on a regular basis the despatch department should run a sequence check of orders received. Where there are gaps in the sequence, they should be investigated to identify any missing orders.
Customers are able to place online orders which will exceed their agreed credit limit by 10%. This increases the risk of accepting orders from bad credit risks.	Customer credit limits should be reviewed more regularly by a responsible official and should reflect the current spending pattern of customers. If some customers have increased the level of their purchases and are making payments on time, then these customers' credit limits could be increased. The online ordering system should be amended to not allow any orders to be processed which will exceed the customer's credit limit.
A daily pick list is used by the despatch department when sending out customer orders. However, it does not appear that the goods are checked back to the original order; this could result in incorrect goods being sent out.	In addition to the pick list, copies of all the related orders should be printed on a daily basis. When the goods have been picked ready to be despatched, they should be cross checked back to the original order. They should check correct quantities and product descriptions, as well as checking the quality of goods being despatched to ensure they are not damaged.
Additional staff have been drafted in to help the two sales clerks produce the sales invoices. As the extra staff will not be as experienced as the sales clerks, there is an increased risk of mistakes being made in the sales invoices. This could result in customers being under or overcharged.	Only the sales clerks should be able to raise sales invoices. As the company is expanding, consideration should be given to recruiting and training more permanent sales clerks who can produce sales invoices.

Deficiency	Recommendation
Discounts given to customers are manually entered onto the sales invoices by sales clerks. This could result in unauthorised sales discounts being given as there does not seem to be any authorisation required. In addition, a clerk could forget to manually enter the discount or enter an incorrect level of discount for a customer, leading to the sales invoice being overstated and a loss of customer goodwill.	For customers who are due to receive a discount, the authorised discount levels should be updated to the customer master file. When the sales invoices for these customers are raised, their discounts should automatically appear on the invoice. The invoicing system should be amended to prevent sales clerks from being able to manually enter sales discounts onto invoices.

Note: only FIVE required

36 NEW HUMAN RESOURCES SOFTWARE SYSTEM

(a) **Financial implications of introducing the new system.** **(9 marks)**

	Time 0	Year 1	Year 2	Year 3
Hardware	(24,000)			
Software	(20,000)	(4,000)	(4,000)	(4,000)
Training	(30,000)			
Other costs		(16,000)	(16,000)	(16,000)
Net cash flow	(74,000)	(20,000)	(20,000)	(20,000)
Discount factor @ 10%	1	0.909	0.826	0.751
Present value	(74,000)	(18,180)	(16,520)	(15,020)
Net Present Value	(123,720)			

Comments:

The analysis gives a negative NPV, which would normally mean that we should reject the proposal.

However, we have only included costs that can be quantified financially, so only have half the picture. Benefits also need to be incorporated.

(b)   **THREE benefits of the new system and how they could be quantified.**   (6 marks)

Benefit 1	Improved morale and motivation due to more frequent feedback and clearer targets.
	Improved morale should reduce levels of sickness / absenteeism and improve customer care. Assessing this impact in advance of the project will be very difficult. One way could be to benchmark sickness rates against industry averages and evaluate the cost of likely improvements.
Benefit 2	Improved staff retention due to increased chance of promotions.
	In the long run this can be quantified in terms of a fall in staff turnover and associated recruitment costs. Predicting this in advance to enable the project to be appraised will require the results of exit interviews from the past three years to be reviewed to assess how many exits would have been prevented by the new system .
Benefit 3	A fall in fraudulent expense claims as the new system is 'more robust', presumably meaning claims require greater authorisation and supporting evidence before being paid.
	A review could be made of past claims to assess what % are potentially fraudulent and this used to predict similar future claims that the new system would prevent.

Section 4

MOCK ASSESSMENT QUESTIONS

TASK 1 **(20 marks)**

(a) At the end of each day, each showroom manager is expected to count the cash in the tills, adjust for the initial float and reconcile this figure to the record of sales made from the till system that day.

Which of the following activities would be revealed by such a control? One mark for each correct answer. **(4 marks)**

A customer had used a promotional voucher to buy a discounted air filter	Yes/No
A customer had paid for some oil using a credit card but the till operator had accidentally classified it as a cash sale.	Yes/No
A stolen credit card had been used by a customer	Yes/No
A member of staff had borrowed some cash, intending to return it later	Yes/No

(b) **Who has the statutory duty to prepare accounts for AEM Ltd?** **(2 marks)**

The company auditors.	
The directors of the company.	
The Financial Controller.	
Companies House.	

(c) The Accounts Payable Clerk has asked you to show whether the following errors would be detected by reconciling the accounts payable ledger to the accounts payable control account.

Tick whether the errors shown would be detected or not **(5 marks)**

	Yes	No
A pricing error was spotted in a purchase invoice		
The wrong percentage quantity discount was calculated on an invoice		
A purchase invoice was debited to the supplier's account		
A purchase invoice was posted to the wrong supplier account		
VAT on a purchase invoice was posted to sundry expenses instead of the VAT control a/c.		

(d) Entry to the receivables ledger is protected by a password.

Which of the following passwords is the most secure? **(2 marks)**

Creditors365	
Veganburger	
246810	
KlerK7&%1	

(e) One of your roles within AEM Ltd is to help choose suitable suppliers. Evan Crabb has written you an email encouraging you to choose his firm as a supplier. Included in the email is the following sentence:

"I seem to have some spare tickets to the upcoming rugby international match and wondered if you would like to have them, as I gather that you are a rugby fan." **(4 marks)**

Which of the fundamental principles of ethical behaviour does this most threaten?

Confidentiality	
Objectivity	
Professional competence and due care	

What action should be taken?

You can accept but must advise the auditors	
You can accept but must advise your manager	
You must decline	

(f) **Which THREE of the following internal control procedures would be most effective for AEM Ltd in reducing the risk of fraud by showroom staff?** **(3 marks)**

For each till, the showroom manager reconciles cash to recorded sales receipts.	
Staff have their bags searched when entering and leaving the premises	
All staff have to undergo criminal records checks before being employed	
CCTV cameras watch over all tills.	
The Finance Director monitors gross profit margins for sales via the showroom	

TASK 2 (15 marks)

AEM Ltd recently acquired WV Ltd.

As part of the integration process, you have been asked to review WV Ltd's budgetary procedures and make recommendations.

WV Ltd undertakes long-term planning and 20X2 was year four of this five-year plan. To date, all four years' budgets are exactly as per the five-year plan, and none has been flexed for changes in activity.

You have been given access to the following variance report for WV's showrooms for 20X2 and accompanying commentary from the Operations Director:

Operating statement for year ended 31 December 20X2	Budget	Actual	Variance
Sales volume (number of cars)	756	630	126
	£000	£000	£000
Turnover	15,360	14,100	(1,260)
Variable costs:			
Cost of cars sold	9,072	8,190	882
Fixed costs:			
Labour	2,560	2,680	(120)
Showroom overheads	1,048	1,290	(242)
Total costs	12,680	12,160	520
Operating profit	2,680	1,940	(740)

Commentary from WV Ltd's Operations Director regarding the past financial year

Sales volume fell short of the budget by 17%, compared to a 15% shortfall last year. Our range of quality cars continues to be well-received by the market and we have won many awards, so it is disappointing that sales targets have not been met.

We put up prices to support our high quality brand, opened longer during evenings and at weekends, and imposed a new system of sales targets for staff. Despite all this, the growth in sales has yet to materialise.

There were, however, some significant cost savings, so the fall in profit was not as bad as it could have been. In particular, the purchase cost of cars sold was less than budget, reflecting good bargaining skills from our purchasing team..

During 20X1, the company experienced some difficulty in employing enough labour to work in the showrooms, so at the end of 20X1 we incorporated more shift work and flexible working.

Unfortunately other showroom overheads increased but we are not sure why.

(a) Evaluate and make recommendations for improving WV Ltd's approach to planning and budgetary control. (8 marks)

(b) Evaluate the Operations Director's explanations of the variances, giving revised variances where appropriate. (7 marks)

(15 marks)

(a)   **Planning and Budgetary Control**   **(8 marks)**

(b)   **Variances**   **(7 marks)**

(a)   **Planning and Budgetary Control**

TASK 3 (15 marks)

You have been asked to review the purchase and payables system at WV Ltd.

Extract of purchases and payables system

WV Ltd has four showrooms. Each showroom manager has a small team working for them and is responsible for ordering inventory of spare parts and consumables for their showrooms. Each week a showroom manager will raise a purchase requisition form, which is sent to the Purchasing Manager, Binny Hameer. Binny consolidates the orders, chooses suppliers and places the orders. He sends any individual orders above £1,000 for authorisation from the Finance Director, Jenny Ng. A copy of the resulting purchase order for each product line is then emailed to each manager.

Receipts of goods from suppliers are processed by staff in each showroom team, depending on who is free at the time. Ideally the purchase order has been printed off by the showroom manager, so the member of staff can check quantity and quality of goods against it. Unfortunately, this does not always happen. What does happen is that members of staff will complete a sequentially numbered blank goods received note (GRN). The GRNs are sent to the accounts department every two weeks for processing.

On receipt of the purchase invoice from the supplier, an accounts clerk matches it to the GRN. The invoice is then sent to the Purchasing Manager, Binny Hameer, who processes it for payment. The Finance Director is given the total amount of the payments list, which she authorises and then processes the bank payments. Due to staff shortages in the accounts department, supplier statement reconciliations are no longer performed.

Use the answer spaces overleaf as follows:

- **Identify and explain five weaknesses from the above system description**

- **For each weakness briefly explain the effect it could have on the company**

Weakness	Effect of Weakness

TASK 4 (15 marks)

As part of a plan to integrate the activities of AEM Ltd and WV Ltd, the Board of AEM Ltd are considering closing WV Ltd's existing car warehouse and expanding AEM Ltd's site to accommodate the increase in car numbers.

William Glass, Operations Director, has produced the following schedule of costs and benefits of the move but you have been asked to consider the approach and report back.

Item	Notes	Impact of closure
Research costs	Cost incurred to date in researching the different options concerning closure. This has cost £3,000 to date including director's time.	Cost of £3,000
Rent and rates	WV's existing warehouse is rented for £96,000 per annum. The lease comes to an end shortly and WV will be able to exit. Additional rent to expand AEM's warehouse will be £72,000 per annum.	Saving of £24,000
Wages	While some existing WV Ltd staff will be able to move premises, some will have to be made redundant or take early retirement. Warehouse staff costs of £120,000 are expected once the move takes place.	Cost of £120,000
Warehouse operating expenses	Operating expenses in WV's existing warehouse are £34,000 (including £5,000 of apportioned overheads). In AEM's warehouse operating expenses are expected to increase by £24,000 (including £4,000 of apportioned overheads) as a result of the expansion.	Saving of £10,000
Existing Equipment	Most of WV's existing warehouse equipment, such as shelving units, will be sold. This equipment currently has a net book value of £16,000 and will be sold for an estimated £10,000. There will thus be a loss on disposal of £6,000.	Loss of £6,000

You have been asked to review this analysis using the principles of relevant costing to help ensure that the correct decision is made.

Use the answer spaces overleaf as follows:

- **Briefly explain the principles behind relevant cash flows for decision making.** (3 marks)

- **Comment on each of the costs above as to whether the figures given for the impact are correct.** (12 marks)

(15 marks)

Relevant cash flow principles

Item	Comment on treatment
Research costs	
Rent and rates	
Wages	

Item	Comment on treatment
Warehouse operating expenses	
Equipment loss on disposal	

TASK 5
(20 marks)

The directors of AEM are considering other ways to achieve high growth that do not involve acquisitions. One option being discussed would be to open new showrooms and operations in Ireland using a franchising model.

Under such a scheme the roles of the franchisee and the franchisor (i.e. AEM Ltd) would be as follows:

- AEM Ltd would acquire the premises. The franchisee then fits them out with fixtures and fittings.

- The franchisee would pay AEM Ltd an initial lump sum for the right to use the AEM Ltd name and run the franchise

- AEM Ltd would supply all staff training and marketing, including the website operations.

- The franchisee would have control over day to day operations but would be subject to various quality control measures imposed by AEM Ltd, such as having to use approved suppliers, etc.

- The franchisee would pay AEM Ltd an annual fixed fee plus 5% of its revenue

To help assess franchising as a vehicle for expansion, William Glass, Operations Director, has obtained the following financial statements for a franchised car retailer in Ireland:

Extracts from accounts of franchised car retailer	20X2 £000
Profitability	
Sales revenue	3,945
Cost of cars sold	(2,939)
Gross profit	1,006
Payments to franchisor	(225)
Other operating costs	(584)
Profit from operations	**197**
Assets	
Non-current assets	214
Inventories	113
Trade receivables	15
Cash	380
Total	**722**
Equities and liabilities	
Equity	300
Non-current liabilities – loans	0
Trade payables	397
Tax liabilities	25
Total	**722**

(a)   Complete the scorecard by calculating the missing ratios.   **(10 marks)**

20X2	AEM	Franchise
Profitability		
Gross profit %	28.5%	
Operating profit %	5.9%	5.0%
Liquidity ratios		
Current ratio	2.1:1	
Acid test/Quick ratio	0.6:1	0.9:1
Working capital days		
Inventory holding period	62 days	
Trade receivables collection period	9 days	1 day
Trade payables payment period	38 days	
Working capital cycle	33 days	

(b)   Assess the following statements and indicate whether they are true or false.
    (10 marks)

Statement	True	False
The difference in gross margins could be explained by the Franchisee paying higher business rates in Ireland.		
The difference in operating margins could be explained by the Franchisee not having to pay for marketing costs.		
The difference in quick ratios can be explained by the Franchisee not owning any buildings.		
The difference in inventory holding periods could be explained by the franchisee only stocking the most popular models.		
The Franchisee in this case typically receives money from customers before it has to pay suppliers.		

TASK 6

(15 marks)

Integration of IT systems

Having acquired WV Ltd, the board of AEM Ltd is keen to integrate the two businesses to achieve synergy and make cost savings.

At present the two companies use very different accounting and MIS software packages and it has been suggested that a new package should be purchased that would integrate systems and facilitate future growth. As well as including generic modules covering financial accounting, budgeting, target setting and KPIs, performance appraisal, and variance analysis, the package can also be supplied with a bespoke module to manage buying and selling cars. Furthermore, the new package also incorporates cloud accounting functionality, such as allowing staff to access the system on mobile devices – for example, if a warehouse employee is sick, then they can use their phone to alert their manager, ask colleagues to swap shifts, and update payroll records.

You have been asked to perform a cost benefit analysis ('CBA') of the proposal and to consider some specific implementation aspects.

As part of this you have determined the following:

- AEM will need to spend £54,000 on new computer hardware. This will have a useful life of 3 years before being scrapped for zero net proceeds. Annual depreciation will thus be £18,000 per annum.

- The cost of the software will comprise an annual fee of £15,000, along with an upfront fee of £40,000 to develop the bespoke car management module. It is felt that an additional £10,000 per annum should be budgeted to cover ongoing enhancements to the software.

- Fifty staff across the organisation will each require four days of training upfront to learn how to use the software, and a further two days a year to stay up to date.

- One extra member of staff will need to be recruited to be AEM's in-house expert and trouble-shooter.

- When evaluating staff time, assume a typical salary of £31,200 and 260 working days in a year.

- The way the different modules are integrated will improve data processing and analysis, saving finance staff approximately 130 days per annum.

- The car sales module is expected to improve the interaction between sales staff and customers, increasing sales by £400,000 per annum. The typical contribution margin is 30%.

- There should also be a reduction in average inventory days, saving £10,000 per annum

- You have been asked to evaluate the proposal using discounted cash flows over a three year planning horizon.

Required:

(a) Evaluate the financial implications of introducing the new system using discounted cash flows and the following template, and comment on your answer. **(12 marks)**

	Time 0	Year 1	Year 2	Year 3
Costs				
Benefits				
Net cash flow				
Discount factor @ 10%	1	0.909	0.826	0.753
Present value				
Net Present Value				

(b) Explain, with justification, which changeover method(s) you recommend, assuming the new software is purchased. **(3 marks)**

Section 5

ANSWERS TO MOCK ASSESSMENT QUESTIONS

TASK 1

(a) Which of the following activities would be revealed by such a control? **(4 marks)**

A customer had used a promotional voucher to buy a discounted air filter	No
A customer had paid for some oil using a credit card but the till operator had accidentally classified it as a cash sale.	Yes
A stolen credit card had been used by a customer	No
A member of staff had borrowed some cash, intending to return it later	Yes

(b) Who has the statutory duty to prepare accounts for AEM Ltd? **(2 marks)**

The company auditors.	
The directors of the company.	✓
The Financial Controller.	
Companies House.	

(c) Tick whether the errors shown would be detected or not **(5 marks)**

	Yes	No	Explanation
A pricing error was spotted in a purchase invoice		✓	*Wrong figure posted to both so still agree*
The wrong percentage quantity discount was calculated on an invoice		✓	*Wrong figure posted to both so still agree*
A purchase invoice was debited to the supplier's account	✓		*Only accounts payable ledger wrong*
A purchase invoice was posted to the wrong supplier account		✓	*Both totals still correct, so agree*
VAT on a purchase invoice was posted to sundry expenses instead of the VAT control a/c.		✓	*Neither affected*

(d) **Which of the following passwords is the most secure?** **(2 marks)**

Creditors365	
Veganburger	
246810	
KlerK7&%1	✓

Generally, the more complicated the better, avoiding words, names and strings of any sort.

(e) **Which of the fundamental principles of ethical behaviour does this most threaten?**

Confidentiality	
Objectivity	✓
Professional competence and due care	

What action should be taken?

You can accept but must advise the auditors	
You can accept but must advise your manager	
You must decline	✓

(f) **Which THREE of the following internal control procedures would be most effective for AEM Ltd in reducing the risk of fraud by showroom staff?** **(3 marks)**

For each till, the showroom manager reconciles cash to recorded sales receipts.	✓
Staff have their bags searched when entering and leaving the premises	✓
All staff have to undergo criminal records checks before being employed	
CCTV cameras watch over all tills.	✓
The Finance Director monitors gross profit margins for sales via the showroom	

TASK 2

(a)

> **Planning**
>
> *Strengths*
>
> - Company undertakes long term planning
>
> - Length of the plan (5 years) seems realistic for a car retailer, although it would be difficult to predict trends in electric vehicles over that timescale and WV Ltd may start selling electric cars having been bought by AEM
>
> *Weaknesses*
>
> - Long term plan is fixed – has not been changed to reflect falls in sales volume, price rises or increased opening hours of showrooms
>
> - Fixed plan has led to the sales volume budget for 20X2 being unrealistic
>
> - Targets are imposed on managers, potentially resulting in unrealistic targets and demotivated managers
>
> *Recommendations*
>
> - A rolling 5-year plan would be better (particularly when major changes occur). This would mean that at end of each year, a new 5th year plan would be added in and so should reflect changes in the business environment, such as competition.
>
> - Greater participation in target setting would increase motivation, albeit at the risk of padding.
>
> **Budgetary control**
>
> *Strengths*
>
> - Company is using variance analysis - Variance analysis involves comparing budgeted and actual costs and revenues to produce the differences (variances).
>
> - Should enable "management by exception", facilitating more effective control and use of management time
>
> *Weaknesses*
>
> - Some variances are meaningless in this situation as they are produced against a fixed budget. Obviously one would expect some costs to be lower as sales volume is 17% lower than expected.
>
> - Variances do not appear to be investigated – the Operations Director does not seem to know why a large showroom overhead cost overrun has occurred.
>
> - Variances are only considered in total and not broken down into sub-variances. For example, it would be useful to break turnover variances down into price and volume factors.
>
> *Recommendations*
>
> - Budgets should be flexed for a more valid comparison
>
> - Variances should be broken down into sub-variances to help identify causes
>
> - Significant variances should be investigated

(b) | **Variances**

The Operations Director's comments are limited by the fact that the budget has not been flexed.

Sales variances

- A flexed sales budget would give 15,360 × 630/756 = 12,800

- This would give a favourable sales variance of 14,100 − 12,800 = £1,300

- Having flexed the budget to match volumes, this variance will reflect price changes only.

- The Director stated that prices had been put up but, without further information, it is unclear how this variance compares.

- Furthermore, lower sales volumes may have resulted from higher prices and the combined effect should be considered.

Cost of cars sold

- A flexed cost of cars budget would give 9,072 × 630/756 = 7,560

- This would give an adverse variance of 8,190 − 7,560 = £630

- The director commented that there was evidence of good bargaining skills from the purchasing team but an adverse variance indicates the opposite – the average cost of cars sold has increased.

- This might reflect a general increase in market prices or a change in mix towards selling a higher proportion of new cars. However, it is vital that this is investigated.

Direct labour

- Labour costs are fixed, so the budget does not need flexing. The adverse variance shows that wages were higher than budgeted.

- The director commented that the company had problems recruiting so may have had to offer higher pay to attract enough staff.

- Alternatively, staff may have been entitled to higher levels of overtime for increased working evenings and weekends.

- Either way, it would be better to revise the standard cost card for expected labour costs and recalculate variances to understand more deeply any control issues.

Showroom overheads

- The showroom OH budget does not need flexing, so the variance shown is valid. The adverse variance shows that OH were higher than budgeted.

- The director was unsure why OH had increased. One possible reason is because the showrooms were open more times during the week, resulting in higher lighting and heating costs,

TASK 3

Weakness and effect thereof:

Weakness	Effect of Weakness
Purchase orders below £1,000 are not authorised and are processed solely by the purchase order clerk who is also responsible for processing invoices.	This could result in non-business related purchases and there is an increased fraud risk as the clerk could place orders for personal goods up to the value of £1,000, which is significant.
Goods received notes (GRNs) are only sent to the accounts department every two weeks.	This could result in delays in suppliers being paid as the purchase invoices could not be agreed to a GRN and also recorded liabilities being understated. Additionally, any prompt payment discounts offered by suppliers may be missed due to delayed payments.
GRNs are only sent to the accounts department.	Failing to send a copy to the purchasing department could result in unfulfilled orders not being detected, leading to stock-outs and customer goodwill being damaged.
The Purchasing Manager, Binny Hameer, has responsibility for ordering goods below £1,000 and for processing all purchase invoices for payment.	There is a lack of segregation of duties and this increases the risk of fraud and non-business related purchases being made.
The finance director authorises the bank transfer payment list for suppliers; however, she only views the total amount of payments to be made.	Without looking at the detail of the payments list, as well as supporting documentation, there is a risk that suppliers could be being paid an incorrect amount, or that sums are being paid to fictitious suppliers.
Supplier statement reconciliations are no longer performed.	This may result in errors in the recording of purchases and payables not being identified in a timely manner.

TASK 4

Relevant cash flow principles

The principles behind the idea of relevant costing for decisions

When any decision is being made it can be difficult to determine exactly which figures should be incorporated and how significant they are. The principle behind relevant costing is that we only incorporate factors that are directly affected by the decision and to the extent that they are affected.

For an item to be included it should be:

- A future item: past costs and revenues are known as sunk and are ignored

- A cash flow: provisions, depreciations are not cash flow and should be excluded

- An incremental amount

  If, for example, we are comparing two possible outcomes:

  Cash position if we go ahead with the proposal   £A

  Cash position if we reject the proposal   £B

The relevant cash flow is the 'future incremental cash flow' and is the difference between the two outcomes = A – B

Comments of existing treatment:

Item	Comment on treatment
Research costs	These are sunk costs (past costs) and should be excluded from the appraisal.
Rent and rates	The rent for WV's old warehouse will indeed be saved from the date the lease ends. Furthermore, additional rent on AEM's premises is incremental, so should also be included.
	However, the schedule only includes one year's rent saving. A decision needs to be made how many years' worth of future costs and revenues should be included in the decision (not just for rent). Ideally discounted future cash flows should be used to determine the NPV of closure
	When leases end there can also sometimes be extra payments to return the property to its original condition. These are called dilapidations and are relevant costs that should also be included.
Wages	The staff that transfer will get paid whether we move or not, so their salary is not relevant to the decision to move. AEM Ltd needs to compare the total wages before with the wages after the move to identify the relevant cash flow.
	Any redundancy costs that would be paid if closure takes place would also have to be included as relevant cash flows.
Warehouse operating expenses	Apportioned overheads will be incurred by the company whether they move or not, so are not incremental.
	The true saving is between £29,000 (34-5) and £20,000 (20-4), giving a saving £9,000.

Existing equipment	The NBV is made up of the original purchase price, which is sunk, and accumulated depreciation to date.
	Depreciation is not a cash flow and should be excluded.
	What is relevant here is the net realisable (i.e. scrap) value of the old equipment – i.e. a £10,000 cash inflow.
	Note: no provision has been made for any new shelving that must be purchased to expand AEM's warehouse. This will be another relevant cash flow.

TASK 5

(a) **Complete the scorecard by calculating the missing ratios.** **(10 marks)**

20X2	AEM	Franchise
Profitability		
Gross profit %	28.5%	25.5%
Operating profit %	5.9%	5.0%
Liquidity ratios		
Current ratio	2.1:1	1.2:1
Acid test/Quick ratio	0.6:1	0.9:1
Working capital days		
Inventory holding period	62 days	14 days
Trade receivables collection period	9 days	1 day
Trade payables payment period	38 days	49 days
Working capital cycle	33 days	(34) days

Gross profit %:	1,006/3,945	= 25.5%
Current ratio:	508/422	= 1.2:1
Inventory holding period:	(113/2,939) × 365	= 14 days
Trade payables period:	(397/2,939) × 365	= 49 days
Working capital cycle:	14 + 1 – 49	= (34) days

(b) **Assess the following statements and indicate whether they are true or false.** **(10 marks)**

Statement	Note	True	False
The difference in gross margins could be explained by the Franchisee paying higher business rates in Ireland.	1		✓
The difference in operating margins could be explained by the Franchisee not having to pay for marketing costs.	2		✓
The difference in quick ratios can be explained by the Franchisee not owning any buildings.	3		✓
The difference in inventory holding periods could be explained by the franchisee only stocking the most popular models.	4	✓	
The Franchisee in this case typically receives money from customers before it has to pay suppliers.	5	✓	

Notes:

1 Business rates will be included in 'other operating costs' and not affect gross profit margin.

2 While it is true that the franchisee does not pay directly for marketing, this (viewed in isolation) would give it a higher operating margin rather than the lower one seen here. Furthermore, the statement is also false as the franchisee does effectively pay for marketing via the payment mechanism of annual fee plus a % of revenue.

3 Non-current assets do not feature in the quick ratio.

4 As long as they are competitively priced, one would expect stock turnover to be quicker for more popular car models.

5 A negative cash operating cycle does indicate that cash is received from customers before making payment to suppliers.

TASK 6

(a) Evaluate the financial implications of introducing the new system using discounted cash flows and the following template, and comment on your answer. **(12 marks)**

	Time 0	Year 1	Year 2	Year 3
Costs				
Hardware	(54,000)			
Software costs	(40,000)	(25,000)	(25,000)	(25,000)
Training time (W1)	(24,000)	(12,000)	(12,000)	(12,000)
Extra member of staff		(31,200)	(31,200)	(31,200)
Benefits				
Finance staff time saved (W1)		15,600	15,600	15,600
Additional contribution (W2)		120,000	120,000	120,000
Net cash flow	**(118,000)**	**67,400**	**67,400**	**67,400**
Discount factor @ 10%	1	0.909	0.826	0.753
Present value	(118,000)	61,267	55,672	50,752
Net Present Value	49,691			

Comment:

The NPV is positive indicating that the new software should be accepted.

However, this is mainly due to the expected increase in contribution from selling more cars. It is advised that this estimate be researched in more detail before proceeding.

Workings:

W1: Labour costs/benefits

Daily cost of labour = 31,200/260 = £120 per working day

Up-front training time = 50 × 4 = 200 days @ £120 per day = £24,000

Ongoing training time = 50 × 2 = 100 days @ £120 per day = £12,000 per annum

Finance staff time saved = 130 days @ £120 per day = £15,600 per annum

W2: Contribution on additional sales

Extra contribution = 400,000 × 30% = £120,000 per annum

(b) **Explain, with justification, which changeover method(s) you recommend, assuming the new software is purchased.** **(3 marks)**

Initially it is recommended that the new car management package be used for just one showroom as a pilot to ensure that the bespoke elements work correctly and meets user needs, as well as identifying additional development and/or training needs.

When launching the full package, it is recommended that AEM adopt parallel running. In this approach both the old and new systems are run at the same time. As well as reducing the potential impact of any problems or failures in the new system, this enables a comparison of results and so increased confidence in the new package.

On the other hand, it (presumably) doubles the workload and this can stress the staff. It is often accused of being expensive, as more resource will be needed.